CONTENTS

Organize Your Digital Life

How to Become a Minimalist "Digitally", Build Another Brain and Live a Focused Life without Distractions in 21 Days with Practical Exercises

By Kai M. Jordan

<u>Disclaimer Notice:</u>

Please note the information contained within this document is for educational and entertainment purposes only. All effort has been executed to present accurate, up to date, and reliable, complete information. No warranties of any kind are declared or implied. Readers acknowledge that the author is not engaging in the rendering of legal, financial, medical or professional advice. The content within this book has been derived from various sources. Please consult a licensed professional before attempting any techniques outlined in this book.

YOUR FREE GIFT

As a way of saying thanks for your purchase, I'm offering *the Digital Detox Worksheet* for FREE to my readers.

To get instant access just go to:

http://swenettbooks.com/ Organize-Your-Digital

KAI M. JORDAN

If you want to get the maximum benefit through your organizing your digital life journey, make sure to grab the free worksheet NOW!

Also, when you sign up you will get my other bundles (Decluttering your Home and your Mind) for FREE! That is a total of eight valuable resources to help you reach your goals.

MORE FROM
THE AUTHOR

KAI M. JORDAN

INTRODUCTION

"More was never the answer. The answer, it turned out, was always less." - Cait Flanders

What if I told you there was a way to add years to life that didn't involve exercise or a new diet? There was a way to increase your performance, achieve mental clarity and build more profound meaningful relationships. No more brain fog, fatigue, and psychological pain? There is such a way: digital minimalism.

What does digital minimalism have to do with all that we have mentioned? Excessive use of technology is unhealthy and destructive in more ways than many of us are willing to admit but can sense. Excessive digital use has adverse mental, physical, and life effects. The odds are if you picked up this book, you suspect the same thing because of your personal experiences with technology or the impact of technology on the world around you.

Technology is everywhere, but it seems like all it does overcomplicate our lives instead of simplifying them. You know the pain of opening your inbox and feeling overwhelmed by dozens of emails, the frustration of losing precious amounts of time on your devices instead of getting stuff done, and the pervasive sense of mental confusion, anxiety, or depression. You rarely ever feel at your best, and your relationships feel fragmented, strained, and less connected. The worst part is that even if all this is happening, you can't stop yourself from using digital technologies. You don't want to lose the lure and wonder you experience by engaging with these technologies even when it hurts your relationships, health, and professional life. However, you can redefine your relationship with technology into something that truly works for you. You don't have to live like this.

I have written two books on decluttering the mind and our homes. While the benefits of doing those two things can't be overstated, they overlook something as pervasive and integral to our lives as technology is a big mistake. When things go wrong there, they go wrong everywhere in ourselves. The pitfalls of our relationship with technology can undo or reduce the benefits from all the decluttering we do elsewhere. That's why it wasn't all that surprising when my readers brought up the issue of technology. After extensive research, I realize the problem is way more severe than many readers imagined; It's deadly serious – literally! The lack of conversation about how serious it gets and what we should do to protect ourselves is worrying, so I wrote this book. This book is for people who:

- Want to simplify and manage their digital lives

- Want to improve their focus and concentration

- Want deeper, more meaningful relationships

- Want better mental health and physical health

- Want to be more productive and efficient

- Want personal growth and professional success

* * *

Here Is How We Will Do That

In the first chapter, we will look at why we got where we are technology-wise. We will look at what design choices and business incentives make our digital technologies work against us instead of for us. We learn why we get addicted to these technologies and discuss what that addiction looks like.

In the second chapter, I will help you examine your relationship with technology. Through that understanding of your habits, we can begin any work. We will then spend some time exploring the benefits of digital minimalism.

In the third chapter, we begin to declutter ourselves. We start a 21-day detox, an essential step before rebuilding and redefining our relationship with technology. The second step is self-discovery, building new habits and exploring other activities to rediscover our values – to discover what truly matters to us when all the digital noise is gone. Understanding our core values will help us understand what our relationship with technology should look like. In the final step, we explore ways of reintegrating technology into our lives in ways that help us.

The fourth chapter hones in on the value of solitude. We spend some time detangling the concept from loneliness and exploring and hinting at why digital technologies create that problem. We learn why we need solitude and how we can take advantage of solitude in a world filled with so much noise.

In chapter five, we look at managing social media. We talk about how to completely disconnect from social media apps without impacting your social relationships with those who prefer the option. We will also have a detailed chat about the effects of these technologies on our minds and bodies.

Chapter six is for those who worry that digital minimalism leads to a dull, unfulfilling life. We look at why life becomes better, more fun, and more fulfilling with digital minimalism than without. We talk about how to take advantage of it.

In the seventh and final chapter, we talk about

taking your capabilities to the next level by building a second brain. It's the chapter where we discuss and share apps and principles that will catapult your efficiency, consistency, and productivity.

If you want to transform your life, continue reading.

CHAPTER ONE: HOW WE GOT OURSELVES INTO THIS MESS?!

"Quitting Smoking Is Easy, I've Done It Hundreds of Times." - Mark Twain

Our inability to put away our devices takes people's lives every day. Inattentive driving is one of the biggest causes of accidents on the road, and a lack of sleep often causes it. Another big reason for accidents on the road is being on the phone while driving, texting or surfing the internet. The blue light emitted by your devices makes it harder to sleep, so we sleep later at night and wake up early. Driving while sleeping inadequately is as dangerous as driving drunk. On the road, your brain takes microsleeps, which are moments of lapses in your awareness where your eyes close slightly or fully. What is scary about microsleeps is that most people are not aware of this happening to them at all. It only takes one microsleep at a lousy moment to end up in a deadly accident (Walker, 2018). Our inability to disconnect from our devices is one of the significant reasons behind inattentive driving.

The idea that your digital addiction can lead to your death in traffic is concerning but not as scary as it gets when we consider all the adverse effects of sleeping poorly and inadequately. Insufficient sleep can lead to cardiovascular disease, diabetes, mental deterioration, low life expectancy, weak immune system, mental health issues, and death (Walker, 2018). Now, lots of things contribute to insufficient sleep. However, addiction to technology is one of the primary reasons many of us sleep late at night and wake up early because we have commitments. Unfortunately, our addiction is putting our lives in danger.

The strange part about learning this is how almost no one acknowledges the connection between our digital habits and how some of us are ailing or dying. Our digital addiction is also detrimental in more direct ways. They can hamper our ability to be productive and take time away from building and maintaining healthy relationships with the people in our lives.

Of course, technology is not all bad, and many good things come from it. It is one of the reasons that many of us remain plugged in. Some of us may be in jobs requiring intense immersion within the digital world. We need to remember that some of the promises these technologies make are mere mirages. So, awful stuff starts happening if our relationship with them is mismanaged (or we forget to see these mirages for what they are). The main question we should be asking before we begin to understand our complex and sometimes problematic relationship with technology is how exactly we got here.

* * *

Technological Developments in the 2000s

Technological developments in the 2000s are the primary reason we are where we are today. We would not have guessed just how powerful and life-altering these technologies would be back then. The first of these developments was social media networks, most notably Facebook. Facebook was not an invention in the strictest sense, but it was the first of its kind. Social media networks had existed for almost a decade when Facebook launched in 2004. Facebook's news feed feature, the 'like' button, and its emphasis on simplicity would define the industry forever.

When Facebook launched, the most extensive social media network was Myspace, which had 5 million users. Five million does not sound like a lot today, but it was a lot back then (Hall, 2021). Facebook managed to differentiate itself by making its site more homogenous and clearer to use, which meant it had a more consistent-looking site. That consistency is desirable when you want your product to be easy to use for a wide range of users. Websites like Myspace were highly customizable, but they did not have a consistent look. They became harder to navigate for users who did not know HTML or were not techies.

Simplicity is vital because simplicity lowers the threshold of who can use the service and helps form habits. Behavioural scientists have observed that it is easier to form a new habit when the habit is relatively easy to do. Coupled with that simplicity are Facebook's added features, like the Wall and the feed. The Wall was a place where users could post information about themselves, things that define them, and present them to the world. It is a powerful feature psychologically because it allows users to present themselves to friends, family, and potential connections in a way they never rarely ever get to in real life. The feed was a constant stream of news, thoughts, and information about what your friends were up to, and it was readily available as soon as you logged in. You never knew what you would get at any new moment. Users saw it as a convenient way to communicate and update others on their thoughts, feelings, activities, and interests. It was unique – there was not a place like it (Hoffman, 2008).

Another valuable addition was the privacy controls that Facebook offered. You could tell

Facebook whom you wanted to see your profile or posts so that not anyone who has access to the internet can look you up and browse your profile. The developer community that Facebook allowed to build on its platform made Facebook a lively place with new exciting games and apps that friends could interact with.

Twitter also found its birth around the same time. However, it was initially just a microblogging site where users could post small messages to followers. It was used by corporations, political campaigns, and celebrities to post updates. Because of that, it became a news source for people and many journalists. It also had the same principles that made Facebook a simple design and navigation success. What differentiates Twitter from the likes of Facebook is its short message form, Trends, and its openness. Twitter lets you know what is going on worldwide, while Facebook is good at updating you on a few select people you know or are friended with (Britannica, 2019).

Coupled with these creations were other hardware developments like smartphones—the most influential of them being the invention of the iPhone in 2007. When the iPhone was invented, Steve Jobs did not expect it would be the kind of miniature computer it is today. However, there were signs that it and other smartphones would eventually get there. Steve Jobs was so confident in the iPhone that he said it was five years ahead of its time. The iPhone had vital features such as music and video playback and the ability to download songs and store photos while offering email, calendar and contact apps. Today, our phones have become social media hubs, web surfing, work, and play devices. Internet readiness was another definition faster with Google's search bar built into the browser, and access to Google Maps was found on the phone. There were signs that our phones were moving toward today's compelling devices.

However, the iPhone was the most expensive phone globally at that time. Apple was always good at getting many of its customers to buy its expensive products. However, it was difficult to imagine the smartphone as we know it today as widespread. Google announced shortly after that that they would launch an operating system called Android, and anyone could use it on their phones. Android comes with Google services as default for search, video and email.

At that time, smartphones were considered a luxury. They were not nearly as ubiquitous today, even though millions of people have phones. To get a clear picture of what the situation was like, less than 30% of adults had smartphones at the time. Today, more than 85% of adults have smartphones. Between 18 and 29-year-olds, that number is 96% percent, and between 30-49 years, it is 95%. We expect each other to have smartphones, while in the 2000s, people were surprised to learn that someone had a smartphone – it did not matter what kind of smartphone it was. We did not imagine then that nearly half of us would be spending between five to six hours on these devices (Wheelwright, 2020).

When you compare those numbers with the number of adults who have computers, the number has stayed relatively the same over the past decade at 75%. That makes the adoption and iniquitousness of smartphones very unique (Pew Research Center,

* * *

Today

Nearly half of us consider ourselves addicted to our cell phones. Nearly half of us experience anxiety and panic when our phone dies. Around the same number also considers their phones their most valuable possession. Imagine that. The smartphone is perhaps considered our most valuable possession because it has, in many ways, become the center of our personal lives, careers, and consumption of entertainment. We prefer looking at our phones when on a date than paying attention to our date. We also see similar phenomena whenever people are in the same room as each other or a family eating at a restaurant. On average, Americans unlock their phones 344 times a day which translates to once every 4 minutes. Many of us spend our time bent over, looking at the phone rather than at our surroundings and the world around us.

Today, many of us find ourselves thrust into this world of constant and total immersion and distraction. We did not have a say in it. We feel powerless against the allure and the manufactured desire to constantly be connected, stimulated, and engaged. A few minutes of boredom are so intolerable for many of us that they may qualify as torture. As Bill Maher put it, "Checking your 'likes' is the new smoking." The irresistible draw we feel towards our devices is not an accident. These devices and the apps they house were designed to be addictive.

Psychologists always knew that you could encourage the behaviour of anyone by reward or punishment. It was experiments made by BF Skinner in his Skinner boxes that gave a deeper understanding of the connection between behaviours and rewards. Skinner put rats or pigeons in a box with a lever, water, and food dispenser. He found that the pigeons would learn to press the lever if pressing it gave them food in the dispenser. However, they would do that for an average amount of food whenever they needed to get fed. He also observed that rats would learn that pressing the lever turns the shock off if he sent an electric shock into the boxes. The more experienced the rats are, the quicker they would go to the lever if the shock was introduced.

Skinner began experimenting with different schedules of reinforcements (reinforcements being the food or stopping the shock) (Theodore, 2020). For instance, he would have instances where the food only came out after pressing the lever four times instead of one time. He wanted to determine how quickly the behaviour would be performed and how quickly it would be stopped under different conditions. He found out that when the reinforcement came at random, the animals exhibited addictive behaviour. In other words, if the food came out after they pressed the lever one time, sometimes seven times, and sometimes the second time, the animals "gambled" to see how much more they could get because the results were unpredictable. They responded quickly and took a while to stop pressing the lever. The same designs and conceptions are built into today's modern technologies.

Engineers who build social media apps have an incentive to keep you using these services for as long as possible. The longer you are on the platform, the more they learn about you. The more they learn about you, the more they can serve you ads that would likely appeal to you. The longer you spend on their site, the more ads they can show you. That is how they make their money. So, there is competitive pressure since Facebook, TikTok, and YouTube compete for a limited amount of attention to make your product more addictive.

Apps like these are part of a framework called surveillance capitalism. Surveillance capitalism is "an economic system centred around the commodification of personal data with a core purpose of making a profit" (Baterna, 2021). Essentially, tech companies and others track almost everything we do online partly because they can sell it. I say partly because some argue that the surveillance of our activities online helps companies make better products for us, anticipate and meet demand, making them more efficient. However, nothing is preventing that data from being used against us for the profit and betterment of these companies and others not connected to technology at all. A part of all this data keeps us hooked by personalizing our feeds and other aspects of these services, therefore exploiting our interests and weaknesses.

The most notable example of this is the infinite scroll mechanism. It is such an essential feature of many of these apps that we do not even think about it. Infinite scroll is the mechanism that prompts you to swipe up to see more posts in your feed. You never know what you will get, so the reward or punishment is unpredictable, which makes scrolling addictive. What the algorithm decides to feed you primarily depends on what it has learned about you and other people like you. The mechanism resembles that of a slot machine. Coupled with these measures are design choices that exploit our innate social curiosity. We get notifications that entice us to visit an app. Instead of the Facebook notification telling you what the status says, the notification only tells you that someone you might care about has posted something new. The aim is to get you on the app, not inform you. Compare that to Gmail notification which includes more details when you swipe down; it shows you the contents of the email until it runs out of space. These design choices explain why the algorithms on these platforms are not interested in showing you things chronologically anymore unless you find a setting somewhere. Most of what you get served are algorithm curated updates with a higher probability of eliciting a response from you. Why? Content that elicits a response is more likely to get you to spend more time on the platform; it does not matter if the content makes you angry, happy, or intrigued; whatever floats your boat will be served.

Facebook's "like" button and other iterations like retweets and hearts add a social aspect to that dynamic. Human beings want to be liked and well-received by others. These designs prey on our introductory human psychology to want to be seen and accepted by others. We cannot ignore what other people think about them. People now post and interact with these platforms, not knowing if they will get a "like" or a retweet." If they do, from who and how many.

The influencer/content creator factor is also considered in conservations about our social media usage. Influencers are like friends to their followers, sharing their bad and good moments with them and letting these people into their lives, creating a sense of connection akin to that one may have with a friend. These become a draw for followers and something they could aspire to themselves. It does not matter if those who consume this content take steps to achieve that type of success; it is equally rewarding to fantasize about it or keep their hopes alive. Believing that your interaction with these apps can lead to success justifies heavy usage as much as some people who believe studying leads to success would justify their extreme study habits. However, others can tell those habits are unhealthy and unsustainable. That ignores the fact that many people who try to be that successful on these platforms do not become successful, making putting your eggs in this one basket a bad idea. No one is saying one should not aspire to be successful on the internet; you just have to be clever and honest about it.

These things create incentives to gamble the system to see how much interaction you could get. I use the word "gamble" because it is addictive, and it depends on luck. Most of the time, engagement depends on several things the algorithm decides to do with your content. An invariable reward creates addiction. You sit in a meeting wondering how many comments you got on your post, if people like it or if it was inappropriate and not edgy. So, when you get notification sounds, you cannot resist the urge to drop everything to check momentarily. Checking inadvertently leads to more than a few minutes spent on the platform. We have gotten to a point where checking your phone, among others, is normalized, although some of us fully understand that it may be rude. All this is by design.

So, if nearly half of us feel like we are addicted to our devices, it is not an illusion. Those are the facts. The word addiction gets used a lot, but it helps to define what it means. Mental health experts have studied substance addiction for decades. While not all lessons they learn about substance addiction apply to digital addiction, there are some key similarities.

They note that substance addiction comes in different degrees of severity, from mild to severe. Also, using something often does not constitute an addiction. The use of the substance has to cause disruption in your life, work, and relationships to be considered an addiction. People often want to cut down, but they cannot. They also use more of the substance than they plan. They neglect their responsibilities and relationships. They abandon their hobbies, spending the extra time they gain on their addiction. They also continue to use the substance despite knowing the adverse effects of their use or even using the substance in dangerous situations. Those to a substance also develop a physical dependence.

How does that compare to digital addiction? Let us take a look (Addiction Policy Forum, 2020):

- Wanting to cut down and failing

Many people struggle with controlling their use of digital technologies. Many would like to set a specific number of hours they will spend on social media a day or YouTube but finding themselves constantly find themselves hours on these services,

- Disruptions in personal life

Some people's relationship with their devices has led to less time with friends, family, or spouses. Some find themselves missing deadlines or essential appointments because of their use. There are plenty of stories of people who have fallen behind on work, their school, work or administrative tasks because they are hooked on their gadgets.

- Neglecting hobbies and other things you used to enjoy

I have friends who were avid readers or played sports but started neglecting those activities as soon as they started using the apps most commonly associated with addictive behaviour. You can say that a part of it is life pressures.

However, the hobbies in question had become such an essential part of their identity that it was jarring to see them as absorbed with their devices. Alternatively, when I asked them for a book recommendation, they just said, "Oh my, I have not read anything in a while, but I read this book a while back..." Only to discover they recommend a book they mentioned to me two years ago.

People change but not like this. You do not abandon everything that used to matter to you to focus on things. You can tell it is not what they want because they speak longingly about their neglected hobbies.

- Continuing to use despite known dangers

I have talked about the number of ways that our addiction to our devices is making us unhealthy and killing us on the roads. Many of us know that being on our phones while driving is dangerous, but 34% of us still do it (Wheelwright, 2020). Many people have heard that blue light from these devices is bad for their sleep, but they still cannot put their devices away when they go to bed. Many of us sleep with our devices right next to our heads; we check our phones while in bed. We pass out due to sheer exhaustion. As a result, the quality and quantity of our sleep are diminished.

If you know about all these consequences and still behave in those ways, you might be addicted.

If you see yourself in most of these, you are probably addicted. What if you do not feel bad about it?

To be addicted to something, you do not have to

'feel' like it is a problem. You might well feel like whatever happens as a consequence is worth it, but that does not make it healthy or sustainable.

Your well-being is what matters. Adults do risk and reward assessments every day, and they have to live with some trade-offs because not everything is safe, but some things cannot be traded or risked.

Skeptics would argue that all of this comes as a matter of responsibility. This is true, to an extent. Some accountability is involved, but there is also an element of manipulation here. We have to admit that the idea that we can be in control as much as we think we are while immersed in this world is fantasy. These technologies have behavioural experts behind them, people who understand human behaviour and triggers in a way you do not. These experts are given vast, powerful research tools. They are handsomely rewarded for their expertise and the actionable knowledge they produce for their companies. They also have intelligent algorithms built to exploit your particular personality profile and put all those new insights. They use tricks from all those insights to strike at your psychological blind spots and weaknesses. Much of this happens without awareness. The fact that you are handling your relationship with technology better does not negate that it is severe, and an alarming number of us are hooked on these products in unhealthy ways.

We now know that social media and similar media genuinely make us feel worse. Social media use has been linked with anxiety, depression, and feelings of inadequacy or low self-esteem. We have to consider the adverse outcomes of other effects of social media like wasting our energy and time or seeing harmful/disturbing/obscene content. Social media is also linked to poor academic and work performance, resulting in more bad feelings about ourselves. There is much harassment online, and it sucks much energy and has terrible mental health effects. Sometimes harassment and bullying can turn into stalking and eventually actual physical harm in the real world. Although it will not solve all these problems, it is evident that we stand to benefit if we regulate our use or remove social media from our lives. When you take all of this together, a defence of excessive use of social media, even when it is how you make a living, is not reasonable. It takes a considerable toll.

We underestimate this toll. Say you are at work and just had a good morning, but you still have a substantial amount of work to get done in the afternoon. You think of a talking break, and you open your phone, which, up until now, you had forgotten existed. You notice a headline about some disaster that has struck some country. That is upsetting, but you do not think much of it and log into your favourite social media app, telling you what everyone is up to. You see a few funny, okay, and exciting posts. Then stumble on you that just upsets you. You click on it to read the comments. You hope to at least share your opinion because what you just saw is godawful. Instead, no one seems to share your perspective. Upset, you comment. Put your phone back into your pocket. You shake your head incredulous at what you just saw. However, you just cannot seem to shake it.

By this point, all that work you need to get done takes a back burner. It would help if you shared this with someone at least, someone you trust, to get their opinion. You take your phone out again and share this with a friend on a messaging app. Of course, they share your take, and you are both appalled. That discussion segues into other related topics. They share upsetting stuff they had seen, too, that just looks like this, and now it is your turn to support them. After you are done talking, you put your phone away, but you get another notification. Some anonymous person has responded to your comment on that past from earlier, and they are being mean. The person took a couple of swipes at your profile. Now they think they have an insight into who you are. They have to make a caricature and attack this strawman to 'own' you. You find yourself in an argument that eventually goes nowhere.

After all this, you have gone through several strong emotions, which sap your energy. You have also seen or heard things that leave psychological wounds which can take days or weeks to heal truly. Moreover, you have just been harassed and insulted by someone you do not know who plucked at some of your insecurities despite all they got wrong. So it is no wonder when you try to get back to work, feel exhausted, are inattentive, and find yourself not making as much progress as you had hoped. You are incapable of performing at your best, but you have also lost hours in these interactions. In those hours, precious time and energy were burned. Suppose you do this every day, and often enough, all these effects pile up. In that case, tomorrow's wounds meld into today's wounds, and those hours and energy wasted accumulate. We have all felt this.

Imagine when you wake up with all the energy and the psychological strength you have to be a good person to the people in your life, and a productive person is like water in a clear plastic bag. Your responsibilities and tasks you have to do are like cups on the table, waiting to be filled. Every time you attend to something, you pour some of your water into a cup. Social media and excessive internet use are like needle pricks into a plastic bag, causing small holes where the water leaks. If there are few holes, the leakage is almost unnoticeable because these are small holes, so not much goes out. However, if enough holes are there, they can quickly drain all that water – that energy. The next thing you know, you have less water in your cup for all the cups on your table.

Key Takeaways

- Our relationship with digital technology is unsustainable and unhealthy, going as far as to threaten our lives and general well-being.

- Nearly half of us are addicted to our devices and continue to use our devices in dangerous and consequential positions.

- Our addiction to these technologies is by design.

- Engineers who build these technologies are incentivized to keep us hooked on them because that is how they make their money.

- Tech companies consider and apply techniques to exploit our human psychology when adding or removing features.

- Our addiction technology is consistent with what mental health experts have observed with other types of addiction like substance abuse.

EXERCISE #1

This month, I'm going to ask you to leave your phone at home. Sometimes. For example, if you're going to the cinema, hanging out with your friends, meeting someone for a coffee, or simply going shopping or running errands. Try to leave your phone at home; I want you to realize the exaggeration we give to the urgency we feel to always have a smartphone with us everywhere we go, it's a reality, and you should experience it.

Please write down your comments below..

CHAPTER TWO: LIVING LIKE A MINIMALIST "DIGITALLY"!

"Truth is ever to be found in simplicity, and not in the multiplicity and confusion of things." - Isaac Newton

Even when they embrace a simplistic and minimalist design in the foreground, all new technologies are trying to pitch us on the idea that more is better. Your apps may look clean and straightforward, but they are places that inundate us with overwhelming amounts of more – more information, more options, more tools and more connections. If you do not participate, feel like you are missing out because it sure looks like everyone is benefiting from having more. However, more is always more; more is always work.

Your mind is only ever capable of handling and dealing with a finite amount of complex information a day. Any information we come across, considerations we have to make, or the connections to maintain withdraw energy from our mental budget. So, from the perspective of our brain, more stuff means more withdrawals on that budget. Also, the more emotionally charged or engaging something is, the more it withdraws from our budget. That means different bits of information we interact with in the world will withdraw different amounts of energy depending on their makeup. After a certain number of withdrawals, that budget becomes depleted. Our brain cannot sustain or focus on very demanding things. It becomes challenging to be productive, we make bad decisions, and our creativity plummets.

To make the most of our mental resources, we have to focus on a few things at a time. The more stuff we have to pay attention to, the more our mental bandwidth is used up and the faster our budget gets depleted. I place such importance on our brains because people are their brains, and if we unburden them, we free ourselves. Our brains are where our lives and experience as we know them resides.

Less is better for these reasons.

Suppose you always feel too tired, too busy, or enamoured by digital technologies to deal with other essential things in your life. In that case, you know that your brain is under much strain. You know this when you need to rush a report because you procrastinate. You know it when you make mistakes on spreadsheets or when, no matter how much you try, you cannot bring yourself to respond to all the work emails that have piled up in your inbox. At the same time, you were lost in an internet rabbit hole. You legitimately feel like your brain is fried, and you cannot muster the levels of mental energy you need to get the work done correctly.

One of the most popular tips against digital addiction is disabling notifications, putting your phone on silent, or using apps that lock you out of certain apps and websites. The only apps that are excluded from that treatment are the ones that are important for your normal functioning as a productive member of society. That is excellent advice, but it rarely goes at the heart of your addiction. It does nothing to equip you with the coping skills to overcome your addiction.

Some people think that the more time you spend locked away from your apps, the more you will get used to it, and once you are used to it, you will not ever have to worry about relapsing. That is inaccurate because you have developed no skills to deal with and manage your usage. I am not saying that these tools are useless; they work best in a more significant effort that adopts other techniques and skills.

Think back to your own experience. How often have you heard a friend or someone you know say they have quit social media, only to see them engage in those habits later? Probably many. The problem is not that these people do not want to change; they do not fully appreciate their situation or spend time building the habits and activities that will protect them from falling back into those habits. Addiction is powerful because it is a habit, and we need to look at what this means to understand it truly.

Habits are behaviours that we repeat without thinking much about them. Habits do not require much effort, and they are formed by the brain when it has mastered a task or done a task repeatedly. Habit formation is a tool the brain uses to simplify and automate a task. When we say they are automated, we mean the behaviour happens without much conscious consideration and usually in response to a conscious or unconscious trigger. Triggers are the things that start the behavioural sequence that is the habit; they are like the finger that presses the button. Like a button can be pressed by different fingers at various times or simultaneously depending on its size, habits have multiple triggers that work in tandem or alone. For instance, getting home from work, cooking or eating at a restaurant may all serve as triggers for a couple of glasses of wine, depending on who you are. Habits are also notoriously hard to change because of triggers and how natural they feel for us. That is why breaking an addiction is not merely about going cold turkey. Reducing those triggers or eliminating them is essential, but what is equally important is developing newer, more vigorous habits to replace those habits, taking the space and the time for those habits.

If you want to stop drinking wine, going cold turkey for a month will not stop you from wanting to drink at the beginning of the following month if the same triggers are still there. You have not taken your time to develop and introduce other options. It is a habit that makes it harder to change and requires more busywork than simply abstaining until you feel used to not doing it.

Our 21-day detox is an analog version of locking yourself away from tempting apps. However, the most significant difference is that you will have to fill your time with high-value activities and adopt new habits. As we have seen, if no work is being done during that time, it will be challenging to stick to your new lifestyle. On top of that, you will be equipped with coping mechanisms to help with your triggers and manage your usage.

Another critical aspect of habits makes cultivating new habits and activities important. I said the point of a detox is to rediscover yourself and your values. Habits happen to create new values. Think about it. When you start a new hobby, you form new ideas about what is valuable, important, or matters to you. The process happens intuitively. For instance, before you get into the habit of growing house plants, it is easy to overlook their value or what they can mean for the owner who takes care of them: the information they retain by growing, the history and sentimental value of this one plant or another. That impacts changing one's values or what is important to them. That is how the value-creating mechanism of habits/ hobbies works. In a sense, they can transform your identity and thus influence your behaviour, where you want to get at. All the things you will be doing in the detox phase are working towards that end goal, not just going cold turkey.

❋ ❋ ❋

Something You Should Do Now

A big part of working on our problematic usage is deeply understanding our relationship with these apps. Why we, personally, are using these apps. The aim of cultivating understanding is to have a clear map or recipe about things that will have to change or be addressed to move forward and embrace a new way of living.

Imagine that your usage is like a complicated brand-new gadget you bought. Your understanding of how it works – what your relationship with it is like – is akin to the manual. Only when you have the manual will you understand how the gadget works, not just its specifications. You will also know about what you can do to protect it or damage it. You will know what you can use the gadget for and what you cannot use it.

We need to ask ourselves why we have the apps that we have in the first place. What need did you hope they would serve? Are they fulfilling that need, or have they turned it into something else? What do these apps do? What effect are they having on your life, and what is their benefit?

Moreover, you need to do that now and take your time doing it. Please do not rush this process; it does not have to happen in a single day or two. Take it at your own pace.

For this, open your favourite note-taking app or take a notebook and make a list of all the apps on your phone. Beneath each answer is the previously mentioned questions. I prefer doing this digitally because you are working with infinite space, and you can move things around quickly. Now, begin answering those questions in detail.

Here is an example of what that might look like:

Twitter
- Why did you get it?

I got it to keep up with the latest news.

- What does the app do?

It is a place where people, essential or not, can share thoughts about any topic. It is available for everyone interested in that topic to read. The topics shown by Twitter under "Trends" may be personalized or show what most people in the world/country are talking about at any moment.

- What need did you hope it would feel?

They need to stay informed about all the important things happening around me or the things I genuinely care about with ease.

- Does it still fulfill that need?

A little. I spend much of my time reading people's reactions and updates rather than looking at what accurate news sources say. I also get into plenty of trend-driven rabbit holes.

- What are the consequences of your use?

I waste much time I could be using to learn any of the numbers of new skills I am interested in. Sometimes I get a tinge of despair from all the stuff I see on there.

Something like that could work for any app installed on your phone or computer. The explanation you give does not have to be as brief. You may find that for some apps, you have multiple reasons why you now use them. Some may be the things you discovered while using the app that aligns with your interests. Our usage of these apps often evolves as these apps learn what we like and what we respond to the most. They adapt, and in doing so, our reasons for using them may change. List all those reasons.

Secondly, ask yourself how important those reasons are to you. Are they essential, or are they just things you engage with because they pique your interest? We do this because we want to have a more introspective, honest, and complete picture of our relationship with our apps and devices. Because of that, it is essential to be honest, and stay away from giving idealized answers. Be cognizant of how you use these apps and the real reasons why you might be using them that way, and record those thoughts so you may reflect on them.

As I have said, the only natural way we will shed our addiction is by working on our relationship with these apps, and a part of that is having a deeper understanding of our relationship with these apps. For instance, I once had a friend who started a burner Twitter account. She was a lot more active and genuinely expressed her thoughts without fear of judgment since no one would know who she was in real life. I asked her why she felt the need to do that.

Her answer was simple. She felt that interactions on her real account were lukewarm for her taste and that there were some topics she cared about that she could not discuss without worrying about how it would affect her career. That answer sounds intelligent enough, and I felt there was still something she was not talking about. I asked her why the second time.

She told me that because she was self-censoring on her main account, she did not feel like she could attract and connect with people she felt she belonged to, "her people," she called it. That meant she felt alone in a sea of interactions that meant little to her. Hence, it made sense to make another account where she could hopefully have those meaningful connections.

I asked her if her burner account was giving her that. She thought for a moment, saying, "Not really." Sure, on this account, she could theoretically be more expressive and say what she thought without worrying about her professional life or what the people in her life, like family, would think. However, she was not making those connections. If she found people who were "her people," all of it felt performative. She felt beholden to act a certain way and not express the whole gamut of her personality. When you make friends you like, you have to be careful not to lose them, and a part of that may be hiding some of what you are. So, in this account, she still had to carefully skirt her way through her interactions for fear of admonishment.

The freedom of expression and genuine connection she was craving is hard to find in the real world and even more challenging online. It requires a tremendous amount of intimacy, vulnerability, and acceptance that only makes sense with those closest to you. Those closest to you are also the people you would not want to alienate. So, opening up and being honest in this way with them is scary. My friend's situation spoke to a more profound social anxiety about opening up to those close to them. The issue at the core of her behaviour was her feelings of insecurity in her relationships.

So, I asked if she felt like there was any value to her burner Twitter account? She said there was, but not enough to justify how much time she spent there. Understanding this is one of the most important steps she took to cutting down her usage and redefine her relationship with Twitter.

It would help if you were open to pushing harder and getting deeper into the crux of why you are using these technologies the way you do. To get at the real reason, you will have to look deeper than the superficial reasons you gave at the beginning. You have to ask yourself why at a more profound level until you get at what feels like the right, most honest reason.

Not all solutions, in the end, will look the same for everyone, but I know people who have improved their lives by decluttering their digital lives. People who limited their news to a couple of newsletters delivered to them each day instead of social media applications. People replaced their smartphones with basic phones and relegated internet use to their computers. Alternatively, people who have quit social media entirely but still interact with these devices because they are essential for their workflow. For each of these people, the change was enriching.

They found time to read the books they had wanted to read. They started living a healthier lifestyle, making time for cooking proper meals, exercising, and being active. Some found the time to learn new skills and change careers. Some started a business. All reported having more genuine, fulfilling, and rich interactions with the people in their lives and feeling more connected and grounded.

One of my favourite things they report is an awakening of their inner life. We underestimate how much of our inner life we dull and drown out with the constant stimulation and distraction we get from interacting with all these apps. Our inner life should not be overlooked as simple daydreaming or wasteful mind wandering; it is an essential part of our ability to remain creative, make sense of our lives, and problem-solve.

People who have more time to allow their minds to wander are often more creative and more productive. While their mind wanders, their brain is free to use multiple regions concurrently to work on a problem they are wrestling with. That type of powerful, complex thinking is often impossible when our brains are focused on something because the brain has to direct its resources to the thing we are focusing on. However, our conscious attention is only good at focusing on one thing at a time, and it is not as versatile as our unconscious mind when tackling problems. So mind wandering and letting ourselves daydream or be a bit unstimulated is essential to getting more out of ourselves and connecting deeply with who we are.

Today, many of us have neglected this part of ourselves and try to catch up on all our undirected thinking the moment we hit the pillow at night. That is not effective at all. That phenomenon I just described is called the Default Mode Network (DMN). It is a connected system of brain areas that switch whenever we daydream, think about the past or the future, imagine things from other people's perceptions, and just let our minds think without directing it. You experience the DMN when you walk without focusing on anything in particular, often when commuting on autopilot or lying on your bed staring at the ceiling for no reason. It is also active during sleep.

A dysregulated and abnormally functioning DMN has been implicated in several disorders like depression, autism, schizophrenia, and other conditions. The DMN of lonely people is also more active because they often experience worry and anxiety. So, when people say that they interact with these apps to keep their minds off things, they mean it. However, distracting yourself is not dealing with your problems (Psychology Today, n.d.).

Shedding ourselves off all these apps is not the goal in and of itself; we want to be able to come back at some point and re-engage with technologies that we truly enjoyed and found beneficial. Some of you will not want to do anything like that; some will. When that happens, we need to do it in the best way possible, which means centring that use around our core values.

❊ ❊ ❊

Benefits of Digital Minimalism

Digital minimalism has many benefits, some of which I have already mentioned. However, there is nothing like a list to sum things up. The list below is by no means the rest of the story. At the end of the day, what you will gain will be defined by what you lost due to your use.

Concentration and focus: Living as a digital minimalist will help preserve your mental resources, meaning you will be able to focus and concentrate on tasks like you never had before. All those distractions and unplanned segues into internet rabbit holes will be replaced by an ability to stay focused and make the most of your time. You will be more productive.

Deeper relationships: You will find time for the people in your life, and you will be present when they communicate with you. This is one of the most meaningful changes in my life as I was able to hear and understand those dear to me.

We often think we are listening and attending to our relationships. However, we are barely there and wonder why we feel so disconnected.

Deeper self-understanding: You spend more time with yourself when you strip down all those distracting and worthless pursuits. You rediscover what you like: the things that genuinely bring you joy, your strengths, weaknesses, what matters to you, and your psychology. That understanding is essential in many areas of life because it informs your decision-making.

Sleep and rest: You will feel rested and clear-minded for the first time. You will feel like a weight has been lifted. Much of that has to do with how well you will be sleeping and resting your brain. It is a magical feeling when you have not experienced it in a while, and you will wonder why you never gave yourself the same care. You will not feel tired all the time.

Your mood will improve: After you shed the toxicity of digital addiction and begin to feel the weight lift, you will feel surprisingly happy and content. No more unnecessary stress and worry. Most of our digital addictions do not make us feel good about anything, and they add to our burden, and we feel worse instead of better. Letting it go is like severing a tumour, and you will not believe it.

Fulfilling hobbies: Your time will be filled with hobbies that destress you and leave you feeling fulfilled. These are hobbies you might have abandoned once your addiction started or newfound hobbies. A fulfilling hobby will complete you, and you will never feel like returning to anything less.

Time affluence: You will have time. Today, many of us feel like we are short on time, and the primary reason is all the digital 'stuff' we carry. Considering that time affluence is associated with being happier (Lyubomirsky, 2008), we are denying ourselves a crucial sense of what life should be about. Having time, even when you are not clear about what you will do with it, is freeing and dignifying. It brings back your sense of control. It also represents an opportunity to learn new skills, cross things off your bucket list, have fun, etc.

Key Takeaways

- Our brains are not built to keep up with all the information we are flooding them with.

- You need to have a deeper understanding of your relationship with digital technologies.

- Habits are an essential part of creating new values.

- Detoxing alone will not change your relationship with technology. It would help if you equipped yourself with extra tools.

- We need time to let the mind wander.

-Digital minimalism looks different for different people.

EXERCISE # 2

By applying this exercise, I want you to connect more with nature by taking long walks in this exercise. Walking is an excellent source of solitude. During these walks, you could think about an issue you need a solution for, self-reflect on some aspects of your life that need more attention or enjoy the great weather. Your mind will surprise you with the good ideas and new parts of seeing things when you think about your life with no distractions, just yourself and nature. Make it a daily habit, and jot down your thoughts below.

CHAPTER THREE: HOW TO DECLUTTER YOUR DIGITAL LIFE

"When you are overwhelmed, tired and stressed, the solution is almost always less. Get rid of something. Lots of somethings." - Courtney Carver

The process of decluttering should be fast, not slow. I know that goes against much of what people expect, but it is not that surprising when you think about it. It will be harder to re-create a healthy relationship with technology if you have not figured out who you are without it. To find yourself, you need to give yourself ample chances and let your mind drift from technology-influenced ideas about itself to what has always been true.

Have you ever lost your phone? I have, and about everyone I know has, at one time or another. The first few days are a bit excruciating because you miss a lot. Then, something happens around the second or third day (it is different for everyone). You begin to feel good. That constant background of anxiety and pressure that followed you everywhere when you had your device wholly lifted, and you start to enjoy and appreciate things around you in a way you never did in a while.

We have plenty of insights about ourselves during that time, but when many of us buy a new phone, we fall back into old habits. We forget how freeing and wholesome it was not to be so tied to our devices.

Some of you might worry that after the 21-day detox, the same thing will occur. However, that overlooks something important. Losing your phone is unplanned, but decluttering your digital life is planned and includes various actionable steps to ensure the same pattern does not repeat itself. Here are those steps:

- Step 1: Spend the next 21 days decluttering and quitting all optional technologies.

- Step 2: In the 21 ways, rediscover yourself and find what makes you happy and fulfilled.

- Step 3: Reintroduce some of the optional technologies, but this time based on the core values you discovered in step 2. You will also determine how and when you will use these technologies.

Then after we have done all that, I will give you extra tools to help shape your relationship with technology. See? It is different. Now, let us go through each step.

Step 1: Detoxification

Step 1 is your 21-day break from technology. Detoxification is not as simple as turning everything off, so we must discuss what that means and how to go about it.

You have cut off anything in your relationship to technology that is not necessary. That means no news apps, social media apps, entertainment websites, video games, television, streaming platforms, etc. If you do not need it as a piece of technology to feed yourself or keep in contact with colleagues or family, then you need to remove that app.

You do not need Facebook or Instagram to keep in touch with family members or colleagues. Sure, you can use those apps for that function. However, it is not necessary unless being on Facebook and Instagram is your actual job. You can use messaging apps that come with your phone or call them. Apply the same kind of logic to all the other pieces of technologies that are not necessary to do y or x. You need to do the same thing with apps on your computer too.

Some apps are not strictly necessary, but they are helpful to have. You will need to keep those apps and define how you will use them. For instance, Spotify is a pretty good app, it is unnecessary, but it can be helpful. You can use it to listen to your favourite podcast or playlists when on your commute. YouTube can be helpful, too; while not necessary, you can use it to learn how to fix things in your apartment, learn new skills and catch up on the news.

Let me explain the difference between the apps we discussed first, like Facebook, and apps like Spotify. It is about usefulness vs unnecessary. When I say Facebook and Instagram are not necessary for specific tasks, I mean there are healthier alternatives, alternatives that are less addictive and to the point, unlike Facebook and similar apps. Direct messaging apps that came with your phone or those you installed work better and are not designed to be addictive.

Valuable apps like Spotify are particularly good at what they do, and they are not made to be addictive. Interaction with apps like Spotify can be paired with other activities that help you. YouTube is designed to keep you hooked, but it is also tremendously helpful if you use it the right way. I think you can keep it, but if you have no good use for it, you can remove it entirely.

On your list of apps, there will be many apps that skirt that line between being addictive. Toxic and useful. You will need to experiment and decide which of them you will keep. If you decide to keep an app., you need to define how you will use it. For instance, you may decide you will only use those apps for educational reasons and stop yourself the minute you get tempted to use them for something else. This rule only applies to apps with no healthier, to-the-point alternative.

If you keep an app, like YouTube, and it brings you problems, you should remove it from your collection.

So, what should you keep? You need apps that read documents, apps for your work, and are generally applicable and helpful in your life. Remember, no app is downright harmful or completely helpful. You need to make sure whatever you decide to keep has better than harm.

Since much of our lives are online, there will have to be some casualties. We have plenty of international/virtual friends we interact within these technologies. We need to think deeply about these relationships and decide which are healthy and vital and better cut-off completely or engaged very sparingly.

Friends have a way of encouraging and discouraging certain behaviours. For instance, if you are trying to quit your gaming addiction, it might not be a good idea to keep in contact with your online gaming friends, as gaming is the thing that brings you together. It will be easier to break your detoxification if you do that. If your friendship is that important, it will not go away just because you disappeared for 21 days.

Step 2: Self-discovery

In these 21 days, you will need to fill all that newfound time with activities. If you were afraid of being bored out of your mind, this is your answer. How do you go about it?

First, try things that you have always wanted to do. If you have always wanted to read more, grab a few books that you think you will enjoy and use the free time to read those books. If there is a podcast you have been meaning to get into, use the time to get into it while you do other tasks you have been putting off around the house or elsewhere.

I try to think of this period as a time you will be experimenting with plenty of activities. The point of it all is to rediscover your values and who you are. It will be a good idea to list all the things you are going to try and have at them. If something does not appeal to you, you do not have to force it – move on to something else you find interesting.

Try new sports, visit friends, go to places you have never been, spend time with family, learn something and attend to artistic projects you have been putting off. Just do things and be open-minded.

Some of the things you will try will integrate easily into your daily routine. These are the things you will likely do often. Some things will be rarer, like scheduling outings or activities on specific days under specific conditions, like seeing local bands perform or travelling to specific places. Some of the activities will have a calendar, like sports. If you join a sports club, you will have a clear weekly or monthly schedule.

At this point, do not worry too much about being overcommitted or getting into habits you will not be able to sustain in the long run. Remember, the aim is to have a good sense of what you like and what is meaningful to you outside of technology. So have fun!

* * *

Let's Talk More About Habits

I said you should not worry about building habits that you will not be able to sustain later, but you may want to break some habits or make it easier to keep those habits. Plus, we have talked about how you will need to build some habits. Not all of these habits will stick, but that is okay. It would help if you even were not thinking or worrying about that.

We talked about what habits are; let us talk about how they form and what makes certain habits stick while others disappear.

The first time your brain encounters a situation or problem, it works hard to develop a solution. At that moment, your brain's attention is devoted to that problem. If it comes across the same situation again, the process becomes more accessible because it has learned from earlier experiences. The same situation repeats itself enough that the problem becomes automated. The brain has developed a shortcut for dealing with that situation. You do not have to use your conscious mental resources to deal with the situation anymore. In other words, a habit has formed. The situation that activates that habit is the trigger.

These shortcuts are such an integral part of the brain that they account for 43% of our actions in almost any situation. Almost half of the time, we engage in purely automated behaviours. That means there are often triggers in our environment that we respond to unconsciously.

Triggers come in several ways. Some triggers are contextual. Meaning specific context will elicit certain habits. For instance, entering the living room might elicit reaching for the remote and turning the TV on. Plopping on the couch might elicit unlocking your phone. Some triggers are emotional. For instance, if you feel stuck on a project, you might open YouTube and watch videos, depending on your mood. Some triggers have to do with what time it is. If it is late in the afternoon, you might slack off because it is nearly time to leave work. All of these are not mutually exclusive. Our environments contain many triggers at any given moment. What makes us automatically choose one action over another is the relative ease of that option.

It might usually be that when you feel unstimulated, you unlock your phone and check social media. However, suppose your phone is in another room. You might revert to another behaviour that you turn to when you feel unstimulated, like playing computer games.

Habits often take a long time to form and solidify, and our brains do not wholly forget those shortcuts. What happens when one habit replaces another? The triggers and the relative ease of that behaviour have gotten better than the habit before it. This explains why some habits stay with us longer while others fall away.

By now, you should get a complete picture of how habits function. Your brain encounters a trigger in your environment, your response to the trigger is the habit, and your brain gets a reward. The reward tells the brain the habit has worked or works for that particular context. Putting these pieces together helps us understand how we can form new habits.

In your 21-day detox, you will encounter triggers for your old habits; it will be a challenge. Knowing how habits work will help you stay on course and hopefully form long-lasting habits. For new habits to be formed, you have to make older habits harder to do and new habits easier to do. That means you have to put obstacles between you and the old habits and no obstacles between you and the new habit. Also, the new habit has to be easy, repeatable, and have consistent triggers.

You want to replace looking at social media with reading a book when you feel bored at your desk. If you have done step one, you have already begun with the process because you have removed all unnecessary apps and installing them would be some work. On top of that, you will have to put your phone somewhere where you have to get up to reach and put the book or books right in front of you(closer). When picking books, pick the stuff you are genuinely interested in.

Secondly, you will need to make reading easier. In other words, do not set challenging goals with your reading, like expecting to read an entire chapter in one sitting. Make the goal ridiculously simple, like, "When I get bored, I will pick up this book and read three sentences." The goal is so straightforward that you will experience no resistance. What usually happens when you set a goal that is so simple is that you will not rely on your willpower to accomplish it.

Why is willpower terrible in this context? Willpower is not always there when you need it. If you rely on willpower, you will be inconsistent, and inconsistency is not how new habits are formed. If you do not feel like reading any further after three sentences, stop, you have accomplished your goal. With time, opening a book when you feel bored as opposed to looking at it will be automatic.

If, after you sit on your couch after work, you usually switch on the TV, you can place your remote in another room when you leave for work and place books or cues for other habits you want to try when you come back on the couch or your living room table. In that context, opening the book will be an easier task than going to the other room to collect your remote. You are training your brain to consider and get used to new options of behaviours within old contexts.

Another way you can help yourself develop new habits in your detox period is by removing the triggers for all habits altogether. If the sight of the TV in your bedroom makes you want to lie in bed and watch TV instead of doing something else, consider putting the TV in another room. Without the TV in your bedroom, you make it harder to watch TV while in bed, and you may not even want to do it.

So, you need to identify triggers in your environments that tempt you to engage in your old habits during the detox and replace those triggers with newer ones. After my digital addiction, one of the things I did to help me stick to my detox was to designate a place and area in my place where I would use my phone and put it down in a bowl. I had to make sure it was close to an outlet, so I would not worry about whether it was charged. If I needed to use my phone, I had to stand there without kneeling on anything, and I did not allow myself to take my phone to other rooms in the house. In the places where I used to put my phone, I placed various books I was always interested in reading. So instead of putting my phone on my nightstand, I placed the book there. I did the same with the couch, the kitchen, the desk, and the bathroom. It did not matter to me if I was reading multiple books simultaneously or if I would finish some of them; what mattered was that I was training my brain to associate those places with a new habit.

When I woke up in the morning, I did not look at my phone, and I would read a few paragraphs. If I did not feel like it that morning, I continued with my new morning routine. I got things done faster, and I started to stop being late for appointments. My mood also improved because I was not inundated with a flood of information as soon as I woke up, which can be overwhelming. I felt fresh! You will also have to be creative with what you do to make your detox period easier and genuinely enlightening. One of the significant downsides of only scheduling new activities to find yourself is that when you get back home and those old contexts, you find yourself in a context that will entice you to behave in the old way. Changes will have to be made so that sticking to your commitment remains easier when you return home. That is why I recommend this.

Step 3: Redefinition

In the last stage, you introduce all those optional

and unnecessary technologies back into your life. However, you are careful to make sure each one you let back into your life is aligned with your goals, values, and who you are. That means everything will have to be reviewed against all you have learned about yourself.

The good idea is to let in things that enrich and support your new lifestyle instead of limiting it. That, unfortunately, means that some technologies will have to be abandoned altogether.

For instance, if you have taken up reading as a hobby, it might be a good idea to install an app called Goodreads. An app like that is well-aligned with your goals to keep reading. It has supportive features like yearly Reading Goals, book recommendations, discussions, etc.

You will want to control how you treat the apps you let back into your life. I advise having a two-tier system where the necessary, essential apps are treated differently from optional apps. For instance, disable or silence notifications for optional apps. It is easy to understand this logic; you need to know immediately if your colleague or boss messages you, but you do not need to receive a notification because a friend has tweeted. That news is not urgent and can wait for when you have the time and the space. So, all the essential apps should have their notifications turned on.

In contrast, the rest have their notifications on silent or turned off, and I recommend you turn them off. Do the same with notifications on your other devices, not just your phone.

The second reason you are doing this has to do with the fact that notifications are triggers. Notifications try to activate certain habits; that is why they are there. As discussed in the last section, we want to limit the number of bad triggers in our environment. It is essential if we do not want to fall straight into old habits.

After silencing unnecessary apps, clean up your home screen and your desktop on your computer. On your phone's home screen, remove icons for those optional/unnecessary apps. On your computer's desktop, do the same thing. Why? Icons and desktop shortcuts are affordances which beckon you to click on them. They are very effective at getting you to click on them. Think of affordances as visual triggers for specific habits. For instance, if you unlock your phone and forget why you have, you are more likely to click on an app on the home screen instead of pulling up the full apps menu. It is like how when you log in to YouTube; you are more likely to watch a video on the homepage than the one you went on the platform to watch in the first place. It is a mental trick. Therefore, if you have unnecessary apps on your home screen, remove them and place them with important ones. This way, you are less likely to slip into rabbit holes. On your computer, pay attention to the kinds of apps pinned on your start menu or taskbar. Remove icons for games and other more distracting apps.

We also need to consider how simple we are making the bad habits when we keep their notifications and icons on our home screen. We are making it very hard on ourselves. I like to call this self-harassment because after the detox, not following these instructions puts you in a place where your app's notifications and affordances constantly harass you. It feels like an intrusion, and it can be overwhelming and tiring.

What about those time management apps or apps that block or protect you from distractions? You can get those, too, if you want to protect your peace. I find that Do Not Disturb or Focus Mode to be sufficient. I do not think extra apps are needed as they might clutter your device anyway. You want to make navigating and using your phones as painless and easy as possible; extra stuff does not support that. You also have to keep in mind that solutions like these are time-based and do not give the same lasting, constant benefits of silencing these apps altogether, not installing them first and removing them from your sight.

❊ ❊ ❊

Time and Place

You need to start designating tough times and places where you will engage with these technologies. In the last section, I talked about how I designated a spot where I was allowed to use my phone and then designated all the other areas in my place no-phone zones. You will need to institute a version of that for yourself. There are places where phones should be a complete no-no. You can disagree with me on these places but hear me out first.

You should not use your phone in your bedroom or bed. This one is a complete no-no because of all the harmful effects it has on your sleep. This means your phone should not stay on the nightstand or somewhere in your room that is easy to reach. If you have a spouse, you will need to communicate with them by designating a place, maybe in the hallway, where your devices will be kept while you are in the bedroom. Do other things instead that are not a device or internet orientated.

If you are in a relationship, this will be good for you. If you are single, this will allow you time to be with yourself and rest. Even when you struggle to sleep, the worst thing would be to get back on your device.

The dining table or any place you eat is a no-no for devices. Trust me, you will enjoy your food more, and you might connect, I mean connect, with the people you live with. If you live alone, that is a nice quiet moment to have. You will be amazed at how clear your thoughts are at that moment. A part of reshaping our relationship with technology was so we could have better relationships with others and ourselves. People naturally socialize over food.

The living room is another no-no, with some exceptions. I know this one is contentious because watching TV and looking at your phone go together like PB & J. How else are you going to quickly Google if the actress in the series was in this other movie you saw last year? We like looking at our phones when we feel unstimulated with what is on TV and quickly looking up things as needed, like significant plot points we have gotten in our favourite series. However, I have learned something that has convinced me about the value of focusing on one thing at a time.

Take watching TV, which most people do when they are in the living room (or should anyway). One of my favourite series is Mad Men. When I was watching for the first time, I would also be on my phone. The second time I was re-watching the series, I did not have a phone. I felt like I was watching the series first, noticing nuances and information I overlooked. I was blind to all that information when I split duties between watching and using my phone. When watching shows, nuances and different information matter; that information is often communicated through body language and visuals in quiet moments. The best films will have a lot to say in those quiet moments where it looks like nothing is happening. It is not about a TV series; this affects anything you are watching. I do not want to tarnish my experience by looking away. You want to be able to watch TV and have a complete experience. I am saying that you should pick one thing at a time. If you watch TV, put away your phone and turn off the TV when you are using your phone.

Where should you use your phone or other portable internet-connected devices like iPads? You should designate a spot. The kitchen is fine, and the spot in the hallway where you put your phone when you are not using it. You can be flexible with the living room as long as you do one thing at a time. The bathroom is also acceptable.

If you are driving or commuting, using your device is a no-no. We have already talked about the dangers of this extensively in the preceding chapters. How about the office, home and away? Your phone is fine at your desk, but it is better to keep it in a drawer, so you do not instinctively reach for it whenever you feel like it. If you cannot do that, you can use controls we will talk about later.

Another habit you must develop is scheduling. You will need to schedule times in the day when you will allow yourself to indulge. That time should be demarcated. In other words, it should not be open-ended. That period should also happen in designated areas instead of other areas. The scheduling melds with your typical routine and makes sure it does not take up too much of your time. In other words, do not schedule two hours unless what you have to do will take two hours.

Key Takeaways

- Detoxification from technology should be rapid, not slow.
- During detoxification, get rid of all unnecessary apps.
- Fill the detoxification period with activities to rediscover yourself and your values.
- Build new habits by removing the bad triggers, simplifying your goals and making it harder to indulge in old behaviours.
- After detoxification, you may reintroduce technology in line with your values.

EXERCISE #3

Journaling is an overlooked weapon for organizing your thinking. The act of writing is mighty on its own to declutter your mind from negative thoughts and get your thoughts organized. In this exercise, I want you to write a letter to yourself; yes, if you have to make an important decision, have some complex emotions, or need inspiration. If you couldn't find it, try to jot down your thoughts and write a simple letter to yourself. You will be surprised how things became more apparent and organized, and your mind will thank you for emptying it from the nasty inner voice, start below.

CHAPTER FOUR: ENJOY BEING WITH YOURSELF "CREATE YOUR OWN WORLD"

"Solitude is pleasant. Loneliness is not." - Anna Neagle

The detoxification steps we have gone through have given you a new life. However, that life is better accompanied by other long-lasting habits that will build on and strengthen what you have developed. There is a risk that you might fall back into old ways by not embracing the ways and habits of this chapter and the upcoming ones. This chapter will talk about a bring one: embracing solitude.

Embrace Solitude

Learn to embrace and appreciate solitude. Moreover, solitude does not mean loneliness or sadness; it means being alone. You do not have to be alone to experience loneliness or sadness. The value of solitude is often overlooked, invaded and spoiled by today's hyper-connected world where everyone expects everyone to be always on, whether via their devices or in person. It is baffling to me the extent to which people underestimate the power of solitude. I have earlier alluded to the fact that being bored and disconnected helps our DMN get to work, and that is a good thing. However, a lot more happens when we take a moment to be with ourselves.

✳ ✳ ✳

Why Do We Fear Solitude?

The simple answer, one I have given before, is that people fear that they will experience loneliness. To see how ridiculous that is, we have to look at what loneliness is and what solitude is. Equating solitude with loneliness comes from some belief

that the two are equivalent somehow. They aren't
What is loneliness? There is a simple answer to
this. Loneliness is the sadness we feel when we
are alone. However, I find that description of
loneliness inadequate. If you have ever felt lonely
around people, you know what I am talking about.
That sadness, the marker of loneliness, can be
present in almost any situation. We experience
loneliness when we are with friends, alone, in a
crown or online. We need to look at the moments
when we experience loneliness and ask ourselves
what the common thread is. Because clearly, it is
not the situations themselves which tell us it has
to be something internal.

I have done my research, and I have arrived at
a theory of loneliness. We feel lonely when we
feel like we are being stifled. When we feel like
we cannot be ourselves, honest and open in a
situation. We feel alone, and then we feel sad, like
we cannot relate to anyone. That is what is making
us lonely.
Loneliness is when the self cannot express itself.
So when we are alone, and we feel lonely, we
are not the ones being alone that make us sad.
We have all these cravings for social interactions,
connection, and belonging that we cannot exercise
with anyone who matters to us. The craving
and the want itself are not loneliness; it is the
fact that the craving cannot be expressed in any
meaningful way. If being alone were the cause

of loneliness, simply being with people would be a cure, but as people who have struggled with loneliness will tell you, that is not always the case.

I came across the loneliness monster in college the first time it happened to me at a level that truly mattered. I remember being very involved in meeting people left and right, making friends and being a member of several social clubs and still going to my place at the end of it all and feeling crushingly alone. It was not that there was not anyone to share my living space with; I did. There was no one I felt I could be myself with and everything I was doing felt more like a script. I was playing at hiding myself rather than a way of expressing my genuine self. The minute I found someone I felt I could just be myself with and express all these different parts of myself, that feeling went away.

Many of the actions recommended for dealing with loneliness reveal that it is about self-expressing or the self-being that it needs to be. Consider the following interventions (Scott, 2008):

- Share your feelings

It is recommended that people who are lonely share their feelings. You might think that is so people can help connect them with loved ones or stick them in therapy, but this is not the case here. The tip is recommended as a way of dealing with loneliness. It works because they open up and become honest when people share their feelings. In other words, they reveal a genuine part of themselves to us.

- Develop quality relationships with people who share your attitudes, interest and values

The second intervention shows us that it is not good to be with people or chat with them. Chatting with random people may distract you from your loneliness. However, it does nothing to alleviate your loneliness if there is no connection. It is recommended to build deeper, more meaningful relationships with people who feel or see the world the way you do. Choosing people more like you is because you are more likely to open up and be yourself around those people.

- Volunteering

Suppose you are going to volunteer for a cause. In that case, it will be something you genuinely care about, which explains why volunteering can help with loneliness. Plus, while you are doing the work, you will meet others who share the same concerns. That is why volunteering is so important.

- Online support

Nothing sounds more dangerous than telling

someone suffering from loneliness to find support online or find a community online, but it works. The reason is simple: you will be able to discuss whatever is bothering you or the things you care about with people who feel the same way. Suppose you are experiencing something new, something that you cannot talk to your real-life friends about or your family. In that case, online communities can be a place to understand and be yourself. Thus helping reduce debilitating feelings of loneliness and hopelessness. Consider how many LGBTQ+ teens find spaces online that help them make sense of their situation and find guidance or connection.

-    Attend to your hobbies

The reason here is the same as before. When we go back to our hobbies, we can express ourselves and hopefully connect with others who feel the same way we do. Whatever hobby it is, it does matter if you do it alone or with others, and it can work.

There are many other interventions, including stuff like talking to strangers. We need to acknowledge that loneliness is not being said because you are alone. It is experiencing negative feelings because you cannot be yourself, whether alone or with others. We also should admit that not all solutions to loneliness will look the same for everyone. All instances of solutions to loneliness will depend on the specific reasons behind your loneliness. People are complex, and their reasons will not always be straightforward, and they might require something equally complex to fix. However, if you feel lonely because you miss being at home, just being at home or calling home will help a great deal. If you feel lonely because you feel disconnected, you make efforts to connect and make your relationships deeper.

Solitude has little to do with feeling lonely unless you are truly alone with no one to talk to, like the world has gone through some apocalyptic event, or you are stuck in space. Solitude may coincide with feeling lonely, but it does cause loneliness. Our anxiety over solitude does make much sense. We are so used to being around others, being with others, and surrounding ourselves with noise that we fear that we would be miserable if we were truly alone. We are socialized, consciously or unconsciously, to believe there is something inherently undesirable about

*** ***

What Solitude Does

Having a moment to yourself replenishes your brain. Your brain is not made for constant engagement; it needs time to recover and think clearly, which is impossible if you are always buried in something. The mind can focus and think more deeply, which is increasingly valuable in a world where shallow, low-effort, and generic ideas are the norm. You are more likely to develop creative ideas, insights and a deeper understanding of any material.

People who are comfortable in solitude often understand who they are and what they want. This is simple: the more time you spend with yourself, the better you understand yourself, just like you would the more time you spend with another person.

A deeper self-understanding translates into a better relationship overall because you better understand what your needs are and what you are looking for in your relationships. That understanding enables one to make better relationship decisions.

When you are alone, you can better get work done and concentrate. It does not matter what work we are talking about, and it might work for your job or personal projects you want to get done. Solitude has always been understood as being a friend or mental productivity. When we are around others, the brain naturally works harder to focus on things that require a deeper concentration level.

The good thing is that these concentration levels

are available whenever you are alone; you do not have to be working on a demanding project to reap its rewards. So you will find that when you are alone, you will be able to think deeply about all the happenings in your life. Deep thought is rare because we are often distracted and stimulated, but it can be eye-opening and relaxing.

One of the times that people value solitude is when they have problems to think over. That is because solitude often helps you examine and turnover things more effectively. It helps to get your friends' opinions when you are faced with a problem. However, an equally important part of that is spending some time alone to think over everything and make the best decisions for yourself.

In a nutshell, solitude helps with concentration, productivity, self-understanding, problem-solving, creativity, healthier relationships and rest.

❈ ❈ ❈

How Do You Find Solitude?

Solitude comes in two flavours: being physically alone and alone inside your mind. The two are not mutually exclusive, but it is an important distinction to make. For instance, you can be in a coffee shop and still experience solitude because you are so deep in your mind that the whole world starts to drift into the background. When that happens, you cease to pay attention to much of what is happening. You have found solitude.

What is attractive about mental solitude is that it is often harder to achieve it when you are with someone. When you are with someone, it is not only rude to ignore them and withdraw into yourself, but that person wants to interact with you, and they demand your attention. So in the same coffee shop, you will find yourself paying attention a lot more to what your friend says and your environment.

The key here is that they want to interact with you and expect you to respond. You cannot achieve solitude when something or someone interacts with you, whether via a device or in person. We can use this information to formulate ways of achieving solitude. The aim is to help you have adequate doses of solitude that our minds crave in this hyper-connecting and exciting world.

1- Put Your Phone Away

It would help if you designated times when you do not use your phone. Those times must coincide with times when you do not have anyone to interact with. Do not just put your phone away because you have to talk or attend to someone.

Put it away because you are giving yourself an opportunity for solitude.

For instance, on your morning errands, you could leave your phone at home, so you spend time with yourself. When you go out at night, you can leave your phone alone to have more pockets of solitude. Here we recognize the phone's ability to demand that we interact and pay attention, making it harder to achieve the solitude we want. This also means that when we are alone at home and want to experience solitude, we should unplug and put our devices in Airplane Mode.

2-   Find a Place and Time to be Alone

Another good thing you can try is finding a place where you can be alone. For some people, it is the garage. For some, it is in nature, and others find they can be alone in their cars. Whatever the place is, or places are, find them and make a habit of being there whenever you can. You can be there for as long as it feels right for you; there is no specific time you have to spend being alone. Just make sure you have it scheduled and do it. Find your favourite place and be alone in it.

3-   Turn off the TV and the Internet

If you want to experience solitude in your own home, turn off the TV and the internet. The TV always demands you pay attention to it, and the internet feeds new information to your devices. You might get tempted to read a book, but do not. The point of all this is not to get absorbed in anything, and it would help if you were alone with your thoughts.

One of the things you can do is a journal. Journaling will allow you to interact deeply with your thoughts. Writing is always an excellent way to organize your thoughts.

4- Get Up Earlier

If you get up earlier, you will have more time to be alone with your thoughts. You can also use that time to take advantage of your solitude, be creative, solve a problem, or be productive, whatever it is—getting up earlier works because people generally do not bother each other at those hours of the morning.

You can also arrive early if you still have to go to work. Getting there early will allow you to have some time to yourself before anyone gets there.

5- Eat Alone

If you usually take lunch with colleagues or friends or at the work desk, consider doing that alone. It will be your time to replenish your mind and unwind so that you are at your best when you get back.

I discovered the power of having lunches alone at

the first job I ever had in college. I worked in a small restaurant, so we never took a lunch break at the same time as some of us would have to stay to serve customers. That meant I had to always take my lunch break alone before the lunch rush. I always grabbed the pie and walked to the nearest park; hardly anyone was there then, and I spent the break on a bench eating, listening to bird songs and people watching. Looking back, I realize how meditative all that was. I would return to my job feeling renewed and much more cognizant of my place in the world.

6- Walk

My favourite of the strategies I have shared is taking walks. Whether walking in your neighbourhood or nature, it does not matter. Walking has plenty of health benefits. It is suitable for your heart, burns calories, lowers blood sugar, boosts energy, improves immune function, and helps joint pain and mood.

Make a habit of taking walks every day. You can use that time to reflect on your life and whatever else comes to mind. Do not take with your anything that will distract you from being with yourself. Walking like this is so therapeutic and meditative that I cannot recommend it enough.

Walking is versatile as well. You can use it to run errands if you live near shops and other amenities.

If you do not want to walk around aimlessly, you can–and I do recommend it–plan your route ahead of time.

You can use these strategies as you see fit. How and when will essentially be up to you. Those moments of solitude can be interspersed with activity and engagement; the aim is not to make you a recluse but someone who takes care of yourself. Humans need bouts of solitude. We are social creatures, but that does not mean always being engaged and stimulated.

Key Takeaways

- Our mind needs solitude to be able to function at their best
- A solitude habit is part of the essential you will need to avoid relapse and protect your gains.
- The benefits of a solitude habit are increased concentration, productivity, self-understanding, problem-solving, creativity, healthier relationships and rest.
- Solitude can be interspersed with non-solitude, and to embrace solitude, you do not necessarily have to be alone.

EXERCISE#4

In this exercise, we will try to get you back from the life of virtual connections to more conversational-based life. Keep your smartphone on Do Not Disturb mode (by default). That will turn off automatic notifications; for emergencies, you can adjust the setting to allow calls from certain people (i.e. your family); you can also set up this feature to be turned on at certain times you determine (i.e. work time). Now you can take back control of your phone instead of the opposite; if you need to check text messages, you will have to unlock your phone and open the text app to check messages instead of checking every notification you receive.

Write down your observations after applying this practice.

CHAPTER FIVE: THE SOCIAL MEDIA REVOLUTION

"Being connected to everything has disconnected us from ourselves and the preciousness of this present moment." - L.M. Browning

How you deal with social media afterwards deserves special attention because our relationship with social media is complex. Social media can make us feel good and bad at the same time, and it makes us feel connected and lonely at the same time. It can be helpful and useless simultaneously, so managing it is not simply an act of turning it off—especially today when opportunities and relationships are found and managed online. We need a system that will allow us to take advantage of those opportunities while protecting ourselves from the toxicity of social media.

Managing Our Social Media

First, we need to appreciate that in-person interactions are more valuable and rewarding than online interactions. If we can make them happen more often, we should. That also means we should prioritize them above digital interactions. So, no checking or replying to social media interactions while in the presence of others. Make it a rule to put your phone away with others.

Another change that will significantly benefit your relationships is using other tools, except social media, to contact and stay in touch with friends. Text and call more instead of going into the direct messages of your favourite social media app. Do this more often than updating your status or tweeting.

The third point is to reiterate a similar point made earlier in Chapter 3: scheduling time to be social online instead of doing it on a whim. You can inform the people you will be interacting with about when you will be available. For instance, you can tell them that they can send you messages, but you will only be available to reply between 5 pm and 7 pm. That removes the pressure from you to reply immediately and creates an understanding. You can tell them that they can always call you and send you an SMS if there is an emergency. With rules like these, you will know that any message you get on your social media applications is not urgent, and you can wait.

You have to log into your social media apps to check messages now that you have silenced notifications. The downside of this approach is that you will not be able to get their messages when they reply to you at your designated times, meaning you will have to keep checking for replies instead of getting notified. Thankfully our devices these days help us solve that problem.

Instead of entirely silencing those applications indefinitely, you can use focus modes on both Android and Apple. Focus mode is a feature that lets you silence or blocks particular apps while you are doing something. Users can set their focus modes and edit them accordingly. For instance, you can have focus mode for work. When that feature is turned on, only apps you have allowed to send notifications will be able to send you notifications while you are working. All apps function on the same playing field when the feature is turned off. Focus mode not only silences notifications from those other apps; it makes it impossible for you to access and use those other apps unless you turn off the focus mode profile.

That means you have to set a focus mode profile for work that will turn off once you are done with work. You can also set a focus mode for socializing so that only your social apps will be able to send notifications. You may want to set one for socializing or any other activity so that work or other unrelated activities do not intrude.

I have set three focus modes on my phone: one for work, another for me time, and another for chilling. The following apps are allowed on my work focus mode: email, messages, Slack, calculator, browser, documents, spreadsheets, presentation, reading apps, noting taking apps, voice recorder, Spotify, and app store. When I am at work, I turn the profile on so I do not get distracted, and only work-relevant stuff can reach me. As soon as I clock out, I activate my me-time profile. There is a best times profile that is automated.

To make sure you use these profiles, you will need to set some reminders, so you do not find yourself socializing when an after-hours email reaches you. That means you will also have to be upfront with the people you work with about when you will be available to reply to their messages. Automatic reminders are a good way of ensuring you switch between your different profiles at appropriate times. It will feel a little odd at first, but it will become a habit once you do it enough.

Apple has more features that make the process easier. For instance, when you activate a focus mode, it will be activated on all the other devices where you signed in with your Apple ID. When this is turned on, apps like Messages will be able to notify anyone who contacts you that you have silenced notifications. Another handy feature that Apple provides is Smart Activation. When you are at certain locations, specific focus profiles will be activated. For instance, the work profile will be activated when you arrive at work. That way, you do not have to think about it as much. You can refine this further by scheduling different focus profiles for different times of the day, locations or when a specific app is opened. For instance, you can set it so that the work profile gets turned on when you open Slack. When you leave work, your home profile is turned on.

For those on Windows, Windows 10 and 11 has Focus Assist, which silences notifications according to a profile you choose. It gives you three options Off, "Priority only" and "Alarms only." When the option is turned off, all notifications will come through. When you select "Priority only," specific apps, which you can edit, will be able to send their notifications to you. You can turn on "Priority only" manually whenever you need it or automate it by telling Windows which apps it should allow sending notifications between specified hours. With "Alarms only," only alarms will be able to sound but nothing else. "Alarms only" is perfect when you want to shut everything out except critical alarms for your Calendar or Clock app.

Windows also give you the option to set specific automatic rules. For instance, you can tell it what it should do when you duplicate your screen. You may not want to receive notifications for emails and messages while you are duplicating your screen because, in most cases, when you do that, you are presenting. You can also tell it what to do when you are playing games. If you are a gamer, you may not want to get notifications which may interfere with your gaming experience. You can also tell it what it should do when using an app in full-screen modes, like watching a video. Lastly, it has an option for what it should do after updating the system. All these options can be found under Focus assist in settings.

These options are more flexible than Do Not Disturb, but if you wish, you can use Do Not Disturb Mode as it is easier. What settings go with, focus modes or Do Not Disturb, will be up to you.

I recommend using these technological tools to unburden yourself.

❊ ❊ ❊

Staying In Contact Without Social Media

Some of you may decide that you do not want to re-introduce social media into your lives. That is also a good option that I think can be very powerful and the most rewarding. Those who chose these options might be doing so because they want to avoid the hold and the demands that social media can have on our lives even when controlled. If you decide to go on this path, there are several things you can try.

You can prioritize socializing in the real world with the people who matter to you and ask them to respect and protect that time. Planning an activity or having something to talk about is a good idea. Socializing in the real world can be spontaneous too, so when you have the time, you can be portentous and see a friend or take someone to lunch. Alternatively, you can schedule meetings or outings with friends or family.

The only cost you will have to be willing to pay is your time and effort. Fundamental life interactions require time and effort because of logistics and the number of unexpected things that may happen. For instance, you might have planned to eat lunch with a friend on Saturday, but that has turned into a stroll leading to attending an art event that day and sleeping over. You have to be open to those possibilities and be flexible with your time.

What you gain in the process are a deeper connection and life experiences. Experiences are a great way of cultivating happiness in our lives. It does not matter if the experience itself was neutral or annoying when we had it. It has been shown that the more varied, honest and real-life experiences we have, the happier we become.

Suppose you are very busy and cannot do real-life meetings often enough. In that case, you can supplement those with technology, but not social media. Of course, there are benefits to in-person meetings that cannot be simulated by technologies, like presence, touch, body language, tone and context. However, depending on the medium you choose, some losses may be perverse. Video calling is one example of this. We can agree that in-person interactions are superior, fuller and more nuanced, but that does not mean using technology to stay in contact is terrible.

There are some advantages to using text to communicate that are not there in fundamental life interactions. For instance, you can hold many conversations at once when you communicate via text. You can catch up with your friend in New York while also talking to a friend about a recent trip you took. When you communicate via text, you can easily keep up with what you said and what was said earlier, which can be more challenging in real life. Texting also allows you time to organize your thoughts accordingly and think things over before replying, an opportunity that might not exist in fundamental life interactions.

Voice calls are good at capturing tone but safe because a person cannot read your body language. Depending on how you look at it, the inability to read body language may be advantageous or disadvantageous. Video calls are better, but they cannot replace touch or presence. My point is that all these are tools you can use to keep in contact, and you do not need social media for that.

You will need to inform all the important people in your life about the times you will be able to make and receive calls, similar to the social media scheduling we talked about in the last section but this time for interacting with essential phone tools. For instance, you can set a video call date with a friend at 6 pm after work. Alternatively, you can use specific hours for texting between 5 pm and 7 pm.

I find this method is less distracting overall. It comes with almost zero pressure and surprises that often come with social media usage to achieve the same ends. There is always a risk of getting sucked in or coming across something that sucks your energy on social media. Sometimes, letting the world into your life can be a lot, even for an hour a day. Communicating through text and calls is very relaxing and genuine. When someone speaks to you through social media apps, there is always a sense that they might be doing it as an afterthought or as one thing among many things they are up to on the platform. These communication options do not come with the same feel. They can create a sense of intimacy that is often lacking on those other platforms.

Whereas before, you were happy to let the world in at any moment during your day through social media, you have to be more in control of what you let into your life and when you let it in. You have to be more mindful and deliberate.

❊ ❊ ❊

The Real Effects of Social Media

We need to remind ourselves why we are taking all these measures, which means discussing the real effects of social media on our lives and minds. We have offered a CliffsNotes version of these effects in this chapter and previous ones but let us have a deeper and more comprehensive discussion.

The most surprising thing about research into social media networks, no matter what you have heard, is that most focus on social media's positive effects. At the same time, relatively little attention was paid to adverse effects.

First, let us talk about the way we use social media. Many of us propagandize our lives through social media, capturing only the perfect moments as if our world or existence is perfect. For instance, if I take a picture of myself with friends at a restaurant, we will all pretend to be extremely happy and fulfilled. We do not record or show the parts where we fought—alternatively, the time when you were sad. We only want to capture moments that are perfect or happy. We use the perfect filters and editing techniques and take bazillion photos to capture the perfect mood and aesthetic. Through this art, we elevate the ordinary, transforming mundane activities into moments of transcendence. If we all remembered that, that would be fine.

However, many of us look at social media and feel like other people have perfect, happier, and more transcendental moments more often than we do. Even if we know people cannot be that happy all the time, the perception that they are is enough to make us form an image of their lives which is very different from their reality. They also build personas on social media, hiding any perceived flaws in ourselves and our lives. We do all this for degrees of social acceptance and validation.

The flaw is that any source approval or validation we get is not of our true selves but a version of ourselves that we have constructed online. It is harder to come out as ourselves as those versions become more prominent. The persona itself becomes more accurate, valuable, and worthy of love and acceptance than the self behind it.

We are conflating true happiness with constructed images and presentations. Many of them are staged by people who want to convey a mental state instead of truly embodying that mental state. True happiness is not just about bliss and perfect moments; it is a state that is more nuanced and less perfect than that. A lack of suffering does not equate to happiness.

The worst part about this social media dynamic is that many of us take part in the hope that happiness on social media will translate to happiness in our real lives. For instance, we think if more people like our stuff, which we tweak depending on what people respond to instead of who we are, we will attract more likes and attention, leading to a situation where one is liked. However, what ends up happening is that the person who gets this adoration is not who we are. We have to catch up and live up to that version of ourselves to enjoy that happiness. Such problems used to be relegated to people in the public eye, but increasingly it is us. The danger is creating a society where people are more disconnected. Ironically, social media can isolate us the more followers and likes we get. Digital happiness cannot always be translated to real happiness.

When we create those digital fabrications, we cannot help comparing ourselves to those digital fabrications, feeling disappointed that we cannot be that happy or prosperous. It can be very damaging to our psyche and self-esteem.

Being inundated with images of a perfect and happy life does nothing but make us weaker psychologically and unable to bear the imperfect, dull, and ugly aspects of everyday life. What is normal and expected as part of life now becomes a tragedy or abuse of the self. It shifts our perceptions so that we are more fragile and unable to tolerate the messiness of life. We need to look at the world and appreciate that it is as imperfect as it is with all its dull moments, ugliness and imperfection, which fill most of our days.

The propaganda of happiness and perfection creates unnecessary pressures to be happy, perfect and succeed at all costs. It informs our expectations of ourselves and others. An example of this is beauty standards. Social media can perpetuate the idea that slim women with tiny waists and long hair are more deserving of love and adoration. Men are also victims of the same content, like they need to have a six-pack and cannot be bald and attractive. These standards create pressure for people to sculpt themselves to look a certain way, even if it may not be the best thing for them, given their genetics and body type. These unrealistic standards filter into other areas like work, business, and family.

If you cannot reach and maintain those standards in real life, it can be crushing. Consider the work-life and hustle trends on social media and the internet that glamorize working too much. If one cannot work that hard in their lives and sustain it, they can feel like a failure and like they are not good enough. Those standards may be unrealistic and unsustainable and rarely enters their minds because all they see is other people purporting to live that lifestyle. All the imperfect moments in between all that is being shared are hidden —leading to weird places when our fakery on social media is holding us hostage to impossible standards.

When we create those digital fabrications, we cannot help but compare ourselves to those digital fabrications, feeling disappointed that we cannot be that happy or that successful. It can be very damaging to our psyche and self-esteem.

Social media has a compulsive obsessive side that

comes on slowly and can develop into a full-blown addiction, with people spending upwards of 12 hours a day on their phones, unable to control themselves. When that happiness comes, they neglect everything in their lives. When they put the phone down, they cannot help but keep thinking about everything they have read, seen or heard on social media. The only way these people sleep is through sheer exhaustion. All these people have in common is how unhappy and unsatisfied they are with their lives. The more unhappy you are, the more likely your use of social media will skyrocket. The same phenomena have been shown with usual substance abuse problems like alcohol. What is dangerous about social media is that it puts you in an isolated bubble where your perspective and ways of thinking become so distorted and removed from reality that some have committed suicide. As a result, especially teens.

* * *

Technostress

Social media gives us technostress. What is that you ask? Technostress is a type of stress caused by the excessive use of technology. It is sometimes defined as negative experiences brought about by an inability to adapt quickly to new technologies.

What we are talking about has very little to do with adoption but about the strain that technologies can have on our mental and physical wellness. The strain is primarily caused by information overload, which occurs when more information than the brain can handle at a time is being forced upon it. The best way to think of your brain when it comes to information overload is that your brain has a highway of information with so few lanes of cars it can accommodate at a time. Information overload is akin to trying to create more lanes in a space that is meant for two or fewer. This means your brain works harder to resolve the situation without losing information. However, most of the time, it fails because it simply cannot keep up. Accidents will happen, cars will get stuck, and it will take a while to get the roads ready again (Chiappetta, 2017).

Suppose you use social media all time, your risk for technostress increases. Like other types of stress, technostress has physical and mental effects. Depending on their seriousness, these effects may extend beyond these domains to touch all aspects of your life. Therefore, avoid seeing them too narrowly because your experience of them will not be that way at all.

The physical symptoms are (Chiappetta, 2017):

Increased heart rate: When under stress, your body is flooded with stress hormones like cortisol and adrenaline, which raise your heart rate.

Cardiovascular disorders: your risk of developing hypertension or coronary heart disease increases. This happens because of prolonged levels of cortisol and other chemicals (University of Rochester Medical Center, 2019).

Gastrointestinal disorders: reflux, irritable bowel syndrome, and gastritis can be experienced. Stomach aches are every day for people experiencing elevated levels of stress.
Muscle tension, pain, or tingling in the limbs: when experiencing technostress, you may tense up or experience pain in your muscles.

Insomnia: technostress may impact the quantity or quality of sleep you get. It can put you in a hyper-aroused state, making it harder to fall asleep (Fry, 2020). It is all a result of these stress hormones that put the body in a perpetual fight-or-flight response state.

Headaches: The tightening of the muscles around the head, the eyes, and the neck can cause headaches. Even with technological improvements today, the eyestrain that can result from exposure to technological screens can also be the culprit in making our screens softer on our eyes.

Chronic fatigue: Many things happen in the body

when stressed that mess with neurotransmitters like serotonin and dopamine, essential in regulating mood, energy, and motivation. Also, the constant state of being in a flight-or-flee state can be demanding on your body, and stress also depletes thyroid hormones (Whitten, 2017).

Cervical pain and menstrual disorders: The imbalance that occurs in your body due to technostress can lead to cervical pain and menstrual disorders.

The mental symptoms of technostress are (Chiappetta, 2017):

Irritability: Being irritable as a symptom of being stressed is very understandable and common for most people. People under much strain often feel like they cannot take any more extra stuff that the world throws at them. They already have enough on their plate, so everything else just feels like a nuisance. It is a bandwidth issue. The emotional and cognitive skills one leads to deal with the other important stuff in their lives get depleted quickly by the amount of stuff they are dealing with, so they find themselves unable to regulate their emotions.

Depression: Constant exposure to social media and similar technology can lead to dangerous negative thought patterns and perceptions that increase your likelihood of being depressed. All the stuff in your body, too, can cross the threshold where it becomes depression.

Crying spells: Finding yourself crying because of technostress can also happen. Crying spells do not have to have a clear trigger. It can frequently happen and for varying lengths of time. Some people experience this as the inability to stop crying for a stretched amount of time and not being able to explain why. At those moments, their minds might drift to upsetting things, or they may feel sad.

Decreased sexual desire: In moments of stress, your body experiences increased demands of hormones to maintain the fight or flight response. It begins appropriating sex hormones to meet those demands at a certain point. That leads to decreased sex drive (Scott, Ph.D., 2020).

Apathy: Another way we respond to an overload of responsibilities and information is by deciding not to care about anything anymore. It is not a conscious decision; instead, it is a state we find ourselves in if we become too overwhelmed. The rationale is simple: if everything is necessary, then nothing is important, and if nothing is important, then nothing matters. That thinking leads to a state where we struggle to care, feel, or be motivated about anything. You might know that doing certain things, like paying your bills, is more important than other things, but apathy makes it hard to act incongruent ways with that fact.

You do not have to experience all the symptoms all at once to have technostress; how it presents itself in your will differ from the next person because people are different. Being aware that such things exist can explain feeling lighter and more precise when we are not using technology for long periods. That is because the way we are using technologies is unhealthy, and it causes more stress in us than relief. Even when we try to be on our devices to wind down, that period can be fraught with upsetting scenes or conduct that makes us feel more miserable about life. So, using these technologies for leisure is weird because they are unreliable in producing desired results.

Like we said just now, happiness promised by these technologies is a great marketing ploy that we all engage in. Stepping away and unplugging is a much more reliable way to unwind and clear your head than scrolling through social media or watching random TikToks.

Time Pressure

The amount of time we spend on social media wastes our valuable time. This is a common complaint from many people. Even people who use social media more casually know that they can lose some precious hours online. You can call this procrastination, but I think that procrastination gets a bad rap. What we are talking about is time stealing. When you experience time pressure, you believe you have less time you need to do the things that need getting done. We will talk about that impact on your performance; for now, let us disentangle this from procrastination.

As many people frame it, procrastination is not the opposite of being productive. Procrastination is avoiding or putting off something that needs getting done, whether because of uncomfortable feelings around that thing or difficulty starting the task. Sometimes people procrastinate because they are not motivated enough to start the task. It is difficult to be motivated to do something early when there is a mismatch between the time given and the amount of time. For instance, if I gave you the task to write a report that would take you a day, in six days. Not only do I tell you to write that report, but I also remove more things from your plate so that you have way less to do while you focus on the report.

Because there is so much and the task we have given you is tiny, procrastination is the safer or even wiser choice. You need to use all that extra time to do whatever else you feel like doing and putting off the report. Notice that procrastination does not mean you are spending your time watching Netflix in bed or gaming; it may mean focusing on other work or reading a book and starting on another project you have been meaning to do. In other words, procrastination just means putting things off.

Around that time, you have three days to hand in the report. You will become motivated to work on the project because you have enough time to get it done, deal with any unexpected problems, and look it over multiple times for accuracy. So, procrastination is not always harmful or unproductive.

Time pressure is different. The person who experiments with time pressure feels like they do not have enough time. It is like me telling you to write a report that would make your day in four hours. When that happens, people respond by focusing narrowly on one task. The more stringent and severe the time pressure, the more quality and care is thrown out for completing the task. So, under adequate time pressure, the Focus is maintained to produce the best results, like writing that report in the last three days. However, under severe conditions, the quality drops. When too much time is given, the quality may drop because the person doing the work may juggle it with much other stuff to keep things interesting (Moore & Tenney, 2012).

Social media increases time pressure because it takes much time from us. The plethora of options, rabbit holes, and enticing content makes it harder to spend less time. One may feel like there is not enough time in the world to consume all the content they want to consume. It steals time, but it also leads to a sense that there is never enough time for anything except the unavoidable stuff one has to do, like eating and sleeping. This phenomenon explains why social media often leads to decreased performance at school or work. It also explains why your relationships deteriorate as a result of extended use. We have also noted that poverty is associated with being unhappy. It makes sense.

Key Takeaways

- Digital minimalism allows us to have a fuller and more fulfilling life.
- Some activities cost more than we give even when we encounter them for 'fun.'
- Digital minimalism allows for a fuller and more fun life.

EXERCISE# 5

Do you remember the term *office hours* used back in school, college, or university? We can borrow it and apply it in our personal life too! Determine specific times and days you're available for conversations on the phone or in person. You can announce that to your friends and family members; if someone approaches you by text or on social media and it seems they want to talk about something, suggest that they call or meet you on your available times, which you already set for conversation/meetups. This practice will give you higher quality conversations and improve your relationships with others (quality over quantity).

CHAPTER SIX: I WANT TO HAVE A FUN LIFE!

"Enjoy the little things in life, for one day you may look back and realize they were the big things." - Robert Breault

When they reject digital minimalism, people often say that they want to have fun their whole life. They imply that a digitally minimalistic life is less fulfilling or complete. They imagine their life without their digital apps and habits as so miserable that they could die from boredom. The people in this camp would often speak of how dependent they are on these technologies and services for their lives. That severing them would be akin to ostracizing a part of themselves, a part of their lives. In their defence, there is some truth to the idea that doing so would feel like they are losing a limb.

It all has to do with how our brains function and form entanglements. To understand this, we have to see things from the perspective of our brain. Your brain is in a dark box, and the only ideas it gets about what the world may be like are all the signals it gets from your sense organs. The brain has to somehow sift through all that data and construct a coherent world picture. So, what does the brain do?

The brain begins by making guesses and testing them against the data it gets. It makes hypotheses and tests them. It does this many times over until it can construct pictures, sounds, sensations, and other things of our lived experience. The brain constructs our lived experience.

The weapon that our brains use to achieve this is prediction. The brain constantly predicts what it will see and what will happen. That prediction is not just a guess; those predictions are from a part of our lived experience. As you read these sentences, your brain predicts what the following words will be based on the extensive experience it has reading text. Your brain does not scan each word, and it only corrects the picture you see now when there is something on the page that is unexpected. This means that what we see and hear is constructed by our brains based on experiences in similar circumstances. The brain only tweaks what we see and hear when the information does not fit the model it has created (Barrett, 2018). Let me give you a concrete example of this.

Take out your phone and open the camera. Turn it to record video as if your phone is your head, looking around from side to side just like you would with your neck. Watch the video and notice how when you move your phone, it is as if the room shakes, as your handshakes, and the room slant if your hand slants while holding the camera. While watching the video, you get the sense that the room moves with your hand and what is not in view disappears. Now, let me ask you, why doesn't the same thing happen when you move your head from side to side?

When you move your head from side to side to look on the left and the right, you notice that the house does not shake. When you move your eyes around the room, it does not go in circles as dizzying as it would if you did it with a camera. The reason is that your brain has made a model of your surroundings so that when you move your eyes and your head, you do not feel like the entire world is turning with your head. It is just you are turning. You do not get that shaky-cam effect even when you slant your head a little or the movement of your head is not entirely smooth. It is as if the world is still, and your head is the only thing moving. Why? Because your surroundings are mostly just models in your head that get constantly updated with new information (Pinker, 2015). That model works by asking predictions about where you are and what you will see, and what is the most helpful way of making sense of that data. If something new enters your field of vision, the brain updates the model. Why does all this matter for what we said about seeing social media feeling like losing a limb?

Your brain does not build prediction models of the stuff in your field of vision; it builds models for anything in your experience and only updates them with new information. One of the brain's jobs is to predict how much energy we will need to do specific tasks. For instance, if there is a gallon of water on the ground and you go to pick it up, your brain will predict how much it is likely to weigh based on experience and ready your muscles and all the relevant parts of your body to lift that weight. The only time lifting things is a conscious effort is when we have no idea how much something is supposed to weigh, and we have to test it out. In that way, your brain oversees your body's energy budget, allocating resources based on the various models (Barret, 2018).

Imagine you walk into the bathroom, and there is a gigantic spider in the shower. Your brain will predict that you will need to fight or flee. Based on its prediction, it will fill your body with adrenaline. A fear/terror will come upon you as your brain decides that is the most appropriate right now. Depending on the situation, you might close the door quickly and run or send your slipper flying towards the spider. Your brain has a model for situations like this. It has used various models to predict the amount of energy you will need for the situation and the best possible responses before handing things over to your conscious brain. The fear you feel is all the energy and the physiological changes your brain has started. When those go away, your fear dissipates. However, if your brain is convinced that there may be more lurking around, you will remain anxious and on high alert. All this stuff is based on predictions your brain makes from experience while monitoring your present.

This brings us to an interesting phenomenon. Not only do you have models, but you are also your own experiences and body. You have models for the people in your life, your relationships with them, and your world. Other people impact our brain's energy budget and predictions. For instance, if you live with someone, your brain adapts to them and bases many of its predictions about life at home based on your relationship with them. For instance, your brain might anticipate relief when you get home, and as you walk through the door, you might feel relaxed. If your relationship with the person you live with is not good, your brain makes predictions about all that may go wrong, and you tense up the moment you leave work to go home. As you walk into your home, you might even be irritable before anything happens. When they call your name, you are ready to snap at them despite knowing why they are calling you. Why? Your brain has learned from experience that if they call you, they will probably say something you do not live with, so it keeps you in a state that is ready for a fight.

Our brains are built to be sensitive to others. They have to constantly make models and predictions to make sense of others and prepare themselves to respond to them. For instance, human beings can read each other's emotions because our brains are adept at imagining what it might be like to be the other person in the same situation. When we see someone crying because they lost a loved one, we can recognize and understand those emotions because similar regions in our brains fire up, regions that would be active if we were in the same situations. We understand other emotions by mimicking them mentally inside our heads. However, we do not experience our brains doing this work.

It is hard when people lose a partner they have been with for years because their brains have to start building new models about their lives and the world that do not include that person. It is challenging for 10 or 20 years; your brain has included that person as a significant variable in its calculations.

The word "loss" is an accurate description of what happens. If you think of the models your brain builds to get through each day as one enormous body, then the loss of something is like losing a limb.

Building new, accurate, and suitable models will take time. People who feel grief often report grief coming in waves or hitting them at random places when they least expect it. They are becoming increasingly aware that they are no longer a part of their living model. For instance, they may be shopping for groceries and realize halfway that they have picked up items for the person they lost.

Buying certain items has become such an entrenched part of their living model that they had not considered how this detail should change now that the person is no longer them. Then the grief hits you. The brain has to make sense of who you are, which models work, and which do not rely on this significant change. It takes so long because that person was literally in so many parts of your model; they were a part of you.

One of my friends passed away. I would always be surprised by the number of unexpected things that would pull me back into that place. I would be relaxing and listening to music when a song plays.

The song would not even be something we listened to together or some song she knew. It would just be a song I listen to, and I think, "She would love this." Then suddenly, I would remember that I could not share that with her. I no longer have anyone in my life with whom I can share these types of things. Sadness and loneliness would come over me. The anger would come right after. It is tough to explain this unless someone has gone through it too.

This brings us to digital technologies. They are also a considerable part of your living model. That explains why the thought of being off technology feels like it will be hard and disorienting. The more intense your usage is, the more of a tough time you will have. However, it would help if you had the separation to allow your brain to build newer models equal to and even compete with those of your addiction.

❋ ❋ ❋

Replacing Low-Quality Activities with High-

Quality Activities

This is where it replaces your addictive digital technology activities with high-quality activities. Low-quality activities like your addiction to social media only offer a few benefits that are an enormous expense to other areas of your life. In contrast, higher value activities offer many benefits with the least cost to other areas of your life. One activity of higher quality is not sheer snobbery or bias; it is easy to calculate.

Many of the things we do have some costs and benefits. We intuitively have this idea in mind. When we decide, we always try to minimize the cost while getting the most benefit. It is how our ancestors survived, and it is how the best decisions are made today.

We primarily understand this concept when it is illustrated in economic terms. You would not knowingly make an investment that costs you more than what you would get from investing. If you knew that investing in oil for 20 years would cost money instead of making money, you would not invest in oil. The same concept works with the activities we get up to, but the benefits vary.

The hiking hobby will cost you time, energy, and money, but you will gain a lot more in your health.

All that you put into it is minimal compared to all

future costs living a sedentary life will incur.

Digital media is a massive cost to your relationships, mental health, professional life, and privacy. We waste time and energy on these apps, energy that would have been better spent on other areas of our lives. In this context, what does high-value activity look like?

A high-value activity is any activity that can improve all those areas adversely while costing you less. Let us take hiking as an example.

Hiking will improve cardiovascular health. It is suitable for clearing the mind and lowering stress. It can improve your sleep, help with loss, and boost bone density and mood. The benefits you get from hiking will carry over to your performance at work and your relationships. How? Scientists have shown that exercise improves mental acuity, a quality which is beneficial for your professional life (Medina, 2014). All those improvements in mood will also add favourably to your relationships.

Hiking is also something you can do to create better bonds with friends if you do it in a group. The mental clarity you gain from hiking alone can help create better self-awareness, which helps improve decision-making.

My criteria for high-value activities are simple: the benefits should carry over to other facets of your life. They should not come at the enormous cost of a core area of your life. Your job is to replace your addiction with high activities or lessen the time spent on low-value activities with high-value activities.

When you think about it, digital technologies can be again if our time and energy spent on them do not outweigh the benefits. The same principle goes for typical high-value activities like hiking. For instance, if you hike excessively, other areas of your life will suffer. One more readily a high-value activity than another is their propensity to deliver the best result. Digital technologies have a higher chance of producing adverse effects when compared to high-value activities.

So, what are popular high-value activities?

-    Learning skills

Learning new skills pays for itself in material ways, like getting a promotion at work, and in personal ways, like gaining insight that helps you make better decisions for your life overall. So, using some of your time on social media to learn new skills will pay dividends.

-    Gaining knowledge

Collecting knowledge for the sake of learning itself is also a high-value activity. New knowledge has a way of shaping our perspective, increasing our critical skills, and building confidence. These things can improve our experience in other areas of life. For instance, just learning about classics can help us better appreciate art. The more things you learn about, the fuller and more nuanced your world becomes.

- Making or fixing things

The benefits of making things are that you gain skills while making things. It does not matter whether what you are working on is an art project or woodwork. There is also joy and satisfaction that comes from it that is meditative. You can use those skills to make gifts, fix problems or improve your well-being. Fixing things also saves much money and helps preserve the value of your possessions for longer. The sense of growth and accomplishment that comes from making and fixing things carries over to other facets of your life. It builds character and self-trust in a way that is hard to describe. Self-knowledge and trust in your abilities will help you take healthier risks, try new things and experiments, and understand others.

- Cooking

Making time to prepare meals is good for you, and it will spice up your diet and allow you to eat healthier, fresher foods. Eating well will give you more energy and make you healthier and better capable of dealing with life. Eating is not just for energy but for the better functioning of our bodies.

We need to maximize and improve what we put in our bodies, so we get the most out of our bodies.

-   In-person socializing

Spending time with friends and loved ones is good for us, and it feels great, especially when done in person. The pandemic has taught many of us that lesson. It will help you rebuild relationships you have abandoned and build meaningful, deeper relationships with those around you. Socializing makes us more resilient because we have better support systems. It makes us happier because humans like to connect with others. It also boosts our immune system and improves our cardiovascular health.

-   Reading fiction

The act of reading fiction seems like a waste of time. Isn't it the same as just watching a show? It turns out that reading fiction has some benefits that are not always translated through other mediums. Reading fiction builds empathy and improves your social perceptions. That means we will find it easier to understand others and perceive situations in a way that was not as obvious to us before. The skill is valuable. Fiction also helps with boosting our creativity, which helps us come up with better ideas and solutions for our work.

- Travelling

Travelling exposes us to engaging new experiences. Incidentally, exposing ourselves to new experiences is associated with more happiness. Even when the new experience itself did not make us happy at the time, studies show that we get pleasure when thinking back to those moments and the lessons that we learned. Travelling can also improve our communication abilities, boost our confidence, give us much-needed perspective, and help us get at the true universalities of life.

- Joining communities

Joining communities of common interest will make you happier and feel more connected. It gives you a sense of purpose and direction. It does not matter what that community's shared goal or interest is, and what should matter is that it is essential to you.

I suggest you search for people who have reached financial freedom—people who have built assets that pay them and do not need to work. There is a worldwide movement of people like this, and they value digital minimalism. They are always looking to build, try new things, improve, learn, and travel. They do it themselves instead of vicariously living through it via digital technologies if they like something. I cannot overstate the joy of doing things yourself, and something about it grows you as a person.

This is not an exhaustive list of all the high-quality habits. You can use my criteria to find higher-quality habits for your situation. Remember, the benefits you get from these activities must extend to two more areas of your life.

* * *

So, You Want to Have Fun?

People who look at the world that waits for them when they limit or discard social media altogether with their dread are not just worried about the difficulty of adjusting to new ways of doing things. They think this life is dull. However, living your life behind a screen is not truly living. How would you know how fun, complete, and exciting life can be if you live life yourself? You cannot.

Our addictive digital technologies are time suckers and distractions. They do not enable us to live life to its fullest and grandest. That is not why they were made, and in decision rooms about what features to add or what tweaks to make to these products, there is not a shred of thought given to "enabling life." They are mere afterthoughts to the corporate imperative to grow and create profit. It is no surprise that they are not optimized to improve our lives and interactions.

Until the corporations fix or roll back the worst aspects of these digital technologies, the best way for us to live is to go out there and do it ourselves. I am not saying you should completely abandon low-quality activities like addictive digital technologies. However, you should manage them, just like we discussed in the previous chapter.

EXERCISE #6

Become handier! In the exercise, we want to build a new habit of having a project at home every week. Try to make something or fix something at home every weekend. You can do that by learning a new hobby or skill and applying it. You can start with step-by-step instructions from online videos or borrow a book from the library about that skill or hobby. Examples include gardening, woodworking, learning your favourite musical instrument like guitar, installing light fixtures, or even changing your car oil or fixing your bike. Get creative and follow your passion!

CHAPTER SEVEN: BUILDING ANOTHER BRAIN

"The height of sophistication is simplicity." - Clare Boothe Luce

Technologies are often pitched as a way of fixing problems. If that is not how they are presented, it is often how people think of them. Technologies like Facebook and other social media were seen, for a long time, as ways of connecting the world and making it easier to catch up with friends and all the other important people in your life. You log on to Facebook, and the feed should contain all the information you need to be caught up. That is more appealing than doing something administratively heavy, like calling each of your friends and visiting them. That should be more appealing to you if you want to streamline things.

These technologies have one promise: to simplify some way of doing things. Whether they have succeeded in those goals is if the cost is justifiable to us or if those goals have been surpassed by the need to make profits.

In discussions about how social media improves or makes our lives easier, I often overlook all the complexity and the messiness these technologies can bring into our lives. As I said initially, "more is better" seems to be the maxim these technologies operate by. You have heard of the term choice fatigue, and it happens because of how complex our world has become and these technologies. Therefore, we have gone the route of digital minimalism.

We know that the world we live in is complex and overwhelming without tools to simplify it and help you navigate it. Navigating often means embracing digital technologies, using them in a way that works for you instead of the opposite. The tragedy is that most people do not learn this or use those tools to their advantage. This has to do with design choices that distract us from our goals and a lack of insight from users themselves. Our devices can exist as a second brain that unloads the burdens of our brain and allows it to function at its best state. That best state is when it is focused on a few things instead of juggling many things mentally. The good news is that we can enable that. Below I will share some steps that will help in the pursuit of using technology to empower us in an overwhelmingly complex world.

First, we must appreciate our limitations.

Many of us make the mistake of trying to use our brains to remember and store information, like facts about an article you read or the things you have to get done tomorrow. Our brains may be good at remembering facts and tasks, but they also forget things. Human beings have a habit of overestimating how good their memories are. This is so we will know from companies that they use that bias against us. For instance, how many times have you come across a service that offers a free trial? Many times, I bet. When you accept the free trial, you always note to cancel the service before the trial runs out if you do not like or use the service. As many of you are reading this will attest, you only remember the trial when you get a bank notification about the charge for the service. At that moment, it seems that time has flown by too fast. You might even end up resigning. If you paid for the next month already, why cancel the subscription now. Better enjoy the service for a better part of the month before cancelling and get your money's worth. It is the sunken cost fallacy, and it works so well. By the time you are boiled again, the time has gone by too fast. By this point, you might rationalize keeping the subscription because it is a service you have grown accustomed to.

Just like that, the company has won another subscriber.

How did it all happen? You overestimated your abilities to remember. This is a well-documented fact about how our brains function. Could you have done something not to fall into that trap? Yes.

One of the essential things you should keep in mind is never to pretend that your brain is other than what it is. Human beings do this a lot. We do it when we think our long-automated habits are conscious decisions instead of scripts running without us putting any thought into it. We do it by remembering things. We do it by believing we are not influenced by advertising or marketing. That willful ignorance hurts us instead of empowering us.

The sheer amount of information we encounter every day leads to mental exhaustion. This is often what is meant when people talk about information overload. Humans love information for good reasons. Information is essential to almost everything we do. It has allowed our civilization to thrive. It allows many of us living in knowledge-based economies to be successful. So, we seek information because the value of information is so clear to us. However, there is such a thing as overdoing it. Our brains developed in environments where information was sparse and the need to process and integrate vast amounts of information was not as imperative, so it is no wonder we are struggling and growing anxious and exhausted to keep up. If we want to achieve anything, whether it is building a business or getting a project done, we must consider using other methods to compensate for our brain's shortfalls and help it shine. That is where building a second brain comes in.

* * *

What Is a Second Brain?

A second brain is a way of organizing, curating and storing information for our future selves. It makes it easier to access and utilize that information when needed in its most pristine condition.

Like when you need to do a presentation for work or build a new product. That package will allow you to make the best decisions and be the most effective at whatever task you have. I believe this kind of thing is a superpower that most of us sleep on.

The irony is that humans have known about this power since they invented record keeping. What is a record except for a way of externalizing our brains? They knew the brain makes errors when recalling information from our heads. Storing it on clay tablets or paper was the best way to visualize and protect that wealth of helpful information. Moreover, civilization rose and fell by their strength to capture and maintain accurate records and information.

Building a second brain has genuinely exposed me to the powers of curating, managing and storing your information. Using that wealth of information, I have accurate predictions about my actions and the actions of others. I have quickly and efficiently built finished projects. I have kept on top of my responsibilities while advancing my career aspirations. How do you do this for yourself? You have to accept a few essential principles.

Principle 1: It is Okay to Borrow Creativity

No ideas form in a vacuum. The best ideas are built upon the ideas of ideas, and creativity itself is often an illusion. To understand this, think about what it truly means to be creative. It should mean coming up with something completely new, something not of this world. In other words, to bring into existence. No individual has the power to bring things into existence. The best we can do is rearrange ideas or matter to make things that people before could not have imagined. However, all that creates is simply rearing and redefining existing relationships in the universe. When we say someone is creative, we do not mean they are creative in reality or are coming up with completely novel ideas. We mean, they are making new connections. A process like that necessarily requires the collection, contemplation and integration of the ideas of others.

This means you have to be open to making it a habit to collect new ideas; you can even categorize them. Writing them somewhere or collecting them using various helpful online tools like note-taking apps can help. You can come back to these ideas whenever you need inspiration.

Principle 2: Capture Ideas

Our brains are good at producing ideas, but they are not very good at remembering them. We all know this, but we cannot resist falling for this trap. It is as if a specific way of committing things to our brain is the best way to remember them. There does not exist such a foolproof way for our brains. How often do you come up with a brilliant idea just when you are going off to bed only to wake up the next day without remembering what it was? I bet a lot. It is a waste to have all these good ideas and now store them somewhere safe.

One of the most important habits is jotting down ideas whenever they come to mind.

The advantage of this method is that you get access to the full breadth of all the ideas that pop into your head. That growing body of knowledge only grows and leads to further insights into your experiences and interaction with others. It is being able to keep your best ideas, revisit them and revise them. The refinement process leads to more profound better ideas that lurch your thinking forward. Much of what holds us back is the inability to build on our best ideas. That inability is not because we are unwilling; we forget those ideas.

The tool you will use to amass that knowledge is essential because different tools will have different strengths. They will all fit in with us and our temperaments in different ways. Popular note-taking apps that appeal to different personalities are Notion, Evernote, Obsidian and OneNote. There are many others, so it is not a big deal if these do not appeal to you. When considering an app, you have to think carefully about what sort of collection you want to build. If you are looking for something more traditionally organized, you should go for OneNote. Evernote is much more versatile and will allow you to save sources and various content more accessible. It comes with different templates for different purposes like journaling. Obsidian is people looking for ever-evolving bodies of knowledge, interconnectedness and graphical presentations of their ideas and how they relate to each other. Notion has a high degree of customization and allows for a more workflow-oriented approach. You will have to check them out before trying them. Go with whatever feels suitable for you. If you use a note-taking app to capture your most important and valuable idea, it better be a tool you enjoy using and simple and easily accessible anywhere.

Principle 3: Embrace Idea Recycling

The idea of recycling sounds like a terrible idea on paper, but we do it all the time. Most of the work we do involves borrowing techniques and ideas we have used previously. Suppose there is little similarity between your work project to project. In that case, some ideas, templates and approaches will be applicable across those projects. The inefficient way of idea recycling is always trying to be building something from scratch each time you start a new project. The best way is to reuse those ideas you have used in other related projects in your new projects. They do not have to look exactly like before; you can tweak them or revise them.

The note-taking you will be doing in Principle 2 will help you find those ideas and transplant them into new or related contexts. Use concrete notes instead of mental patterns to ensure consistency and accuracy across your work. If improvements are made in your new projects, you can always go back to your notes to refine them and make them better. It is essential to make those notes grow with you as your experience deepens.

Principle 4: Projects over category

When you build your notes, your second brain, you need to organize them by project instead of category. There can be extensive categories, like active projects and finished projects. However, overall, you need to focus your note-taking on the current thing you are working on. You can draw from other projects or add material from earlier projects.

When projects are prioritized, your note-taking has more direction. It is easier for your mind to work with goals and organize information according to goals. However, it is harder to go with endless open-ended categories. It becomes even harder when you want to use that knowledge for a project. Again, this works better if you want to be efficient.

When you think about it, our brains make associations. They have categories, but they work better when associating the information with purpose. It is even a much more engaging and fun experience for our brain when we sort things for a purpose. For instance, I came into a room and asked you to sort things by their shapes. You would do it, but I do not think it would be any fun or exciting to do. Imagine the same room, but I asked to sort things by the most efficient weapon to the least. You are still doing some sorting, but you have to be more creative and imaginative, which makes the process fun.

I want you to have fun when you build your second

brain. If you cannot have fun, you are unlikely to stick to the habit.

Principle 5: Take Your Time

When working with your second brain, you do not have to quickly start and finish a project. The second brain works a lot better if you take the time to discover and gather ideas relevant to your project. We talked about time pressure and the downsides of rushing things, and it makes more sense that you spend an adequate amount of time on the complexity and requirements of the projects.

I think this principle also goes so well with the second brain because of how well central note-taking systems work to capture more ideas the more time goes by. Not just ideas but valuable ideas, mainly if you stick to taking notes wherever you are and whatever you are doing. As soon as a brilliant idea crosses your mind, even a little promising idea, jot it down.

Different from how you used to work before is how many of the ideas that come to your mind that you discarded get to be used. That elevates your work. In other words, you can produce a product of better quality than you would if you were not keeping a central note-taking system.

Principle 6: Do not Start from Scratch

It would help if you took your time but do not but never start from scratch unless you have to. We have talked about the idea of recycling ideas, and you can use the bones of previous projects to build a new one. You might wonder about the point of taking your time, given that you already started a lot further along than you had when you were starting.

The reason is simple: There is always space to improve and advance, which becomes one way of growing and dancing your knowledge. So not only is the database you have built helping you get things done a lot more efficiently, but it also helps evolve and advance your second brain. It helps you grow faster.

Principle 7: Content Blocks

The matter of how you organize your projects is also super important. To avoid being overwhelmed, you need to divide big projects into manageable packets. It does not matter how complex the projects are; everything, no matter how complex, is fundamentally made up of simple things. The brain is adept at working with simple, manageable information packets.

So, when faced with a project, divide it up into smaller chunks that you think are more manageable.
Then use your second brain to fill those chunks. Remember, begin with the information already in the system, then find and add more information as you find gaps.

Principle 8: You Know What You Know

Do not underestimate or undervalue what you know and what insights come to you without directed research. Directed research is a bit of research because you have a specific goal. So, suppose you are working on a presentation about anxiety. In that case, all of the statistics and articles you go looking for to add to your presentation are part of that research.

However, all the other information and insights you come across each day by chance, like while reading a fiction book or listening to a podcast, may engender some insights that are useful and interesting. You need to record and organize that information in a much-involved way. What do I mean by involved? Instead of just jotting down what your insights were, you can investigate those ideas a little further and add to them.

Let us say that while listening to podcasts on the pandemic, you learn about the various ways that loneliness and social distancing exacerbated mental health issues and also how this difficult time has added layers of direct grief and ambiguous grief to the whole experience. You may gain insights into how the uncertainty of life makes people more anxious and ambiguous or how those experiences often redefine the meaning of relationships. You record those insights and any extra thoughts you might have about them.

You may listen to other podcasts or read material that you find attractive in your spare time. As you do, those thoughts may expand and integrate with older models you had.

Although gathering that information is looser and less centred on specific goals, it creates a wealth of knowledge that may be useful for future projects or the project you are working on now. It is the same process we go through when we learn new things in the world without thinking too hard about it, except you are saving those ideas and thoughts in their most pristine conditions. Later on, when you have projects, you may look to those ideas again to add to your goal-orientated research.

Why does this matter? It makes the presentation of those ideas more original and authentic in a way that speaks to others. It makes more of an impact than dry, goal-oriented research and presentation. It makes your work stand out more.

Principle 9: Live Your Ideas

As you collect these ideas and insights, you need to find ways to apply them to your life. Even when they are purely knowledge-based ideas with no practical application, you can still use those insights in how you decide to view and make sense of the world.

Living your idea necessarily means you will have to revisit them from time to time. Keep looking for more exciting ways of adding them to how you do things when you do. If you cannot find practical applications for these ideas in your life, share them with others who may find them helpful or integrate them into your work to express old ideas in a new dimension.

This principle will help you not just capture and store ideas but truly learn and benefit from them yourself. The 'growing' part of all this work becomes apparent.

Principle 10: Set Reminders

As I have said at the beginning of this chapter, keeping appointments and other essential tasks that have to get done in your mind alone is not efficient. It also creates an extra burden on your mind, making dealing with the tasks in front of you harder.

Keep a detailed calendar of all the essential tasks and appointments you have to get done to free up your brain's resources. Your brain is not good anyway at doing that by itself so relegating it to your second brain and setting reminders is a good way of letting it focus on what it is good at, which is profoundly analytical and creative work, not remembering details keeping track of time. It is one of the most potent ways to de-stress, in my opinion.

Key Takeaways

- The world is too complex nowadays to entirely rely on our brains for everything.
- A second brain is a way of organizing information that helps our brains function at their best and guarantee consistency in quality and accuracy.
- Note-taking is a powerful way of supercharging our brains.
- Reminders help unburden our brain's resources.
- The second brain is an ever-evolving life-changing tool that works for life and our professional lives.

KAI M. JORDAN

* * *

FINAL WORDS

We began the first chapter by admitting some hard truths about our relationship with technology. We learned how excessive use of digital technologies is hurting us. We learned how little sleep and an inability to put our phones down lead to a type of road accident that involves a lapse in awareness that is often not even recognized by the people who experience it. Not only that but inadequate sleep alone has been linked to several adverse health conditions that significantly reduce our life expectancy. You think with all that knowledge, we would opt to make our technologies safer and less addictive, but we did not do that. Instead, companies stand to make more money the more time they spend on their platforms. They use old and new psychological insights to addict us to their apps. Everything, the infinite scroll wheel, notification design, the post we see, and the staff recommended to us, serves to addict us and increase corporate profits.

To understand what it means to be addicted to technology, we looked at how experts have characterized and understood substance addiction. We quickly saw strong parallels between addiction as traditionally understood by mental health experts and digital addiction. Things like an inability to cut down, disruptions in personal life, neglecting hobbies, and continuing to use despite known dangers. We also reexamined how there was no rational excuse for excessive use of digital technologies unless it is your job to do so. We also looked at the argument of personal responsibility. We saw that it is not as strong an argument because behavioural experts are behind these designs, taking advantage of innate human vulnerabilities. These techniques are so strong that even they fall for them, too.

We began examining your relationship with your digital technologies in the second chapter. I advised you to reflect on the apps you have on your phones and ask yourself why you had them and if they are serving your needs now or has your relationship with them evolved into something new, something divorced from what you were looking for. In that chapter, we also talked about what we miss when we are so plugged in. We talked about the ability to let our minds think and wonder, which is essential for our productivity and creativity. Couples with these considerations looked at the benefits we get from living a minimalistic digital life.

We talked about how a digitally minimalist life

boosts focus and allows us to form and maintain more profound and meaningful relationships. We talked about how it leads to even better self-understanding, which leads to maturity. Maturity is all about making the best decisions for yourself and knowing how you will interact with all around you. Another fruit of a digitally minimalistic life is building life-enriching hobbies. Even discovering old hobbies you used to enjoy is also magical because it helps you rediscover and gain more insight into yourself. What matters is how, overall, these hobbies are more fulfilling. Digital minimalism helps us truly rest and sleep, probably adding years to our lives and improving or helping with the functions of every organ in our body. Sleep is so powerful that it is difficult to think of a part of ourselves that does not impact. It is no wonder that our moods and mental health improve with digital minimalism. Another gift so prized in our super busy lives is time affluence. We find ourselves with more time to do what we consider best—no more feeling like we do not have enough.

In the third chapter, we delved into ways of decluttering our digital lives. We talk about differentiating between necessary, helpful, and unnecessary apps for the first time. We learned that unnecessary apps had to be purged for 21 days. In the second step, we talked about what should be done during that time. We talked about how one should do new and exciting things or build new habits. At this point, we started learning about the nature of habits. Those habits are automatic scripts that are built through repetition and experience. They are there because the mind is very good at simplifying things. We saw that the easiest and most triggered habits tend to stay, which made us think of more clever ways to help us stick to our 21-day detox. We talked about how we should use old triggers to form new behaviours or remove old triggers. This part of the process was perhaps the most useful in staying off our technology. Because of this discussion, we talk about the importance of triggers and making rules to combat them. We also talk about the importance of redefining or rediscovering yourself at this time.

Then we devoted an entire chapter to solitude because solitude is boss if I am honest. However, before we got to how boss and excellent solitude is, we had to disentangle it from misconceptions people have about solitude, as solitudes equate to loneliness. In doing that, we learned a lot about what loneliness truly is, and, as we found out, it had very little to do with solitude. That taught us a lot about what the self is, what it wants and how that should be treated. I also think that we got to appreciate the importance of self-expression and honesty overall in that process. We learned how to deal with loneliness before talking about all the awesome things that solitude does for us. We know that solitude is in short supply because of its misconceptions and how our world today tries to crowd out any bits of private moments it can find. We learned that

Solitude is as precious as it is rare nowadays, and I got some excellent tips on attaining it and regularly practicing it. In my opinion, there is little separating solitude and meditation.

After we learned how you could detoxify, learn new habits, and embrace solitude, we talked about a way of keeping up with friends and reconnecting. We talked about how introducing old digital habits should be handled. The importance of scheduling, silencing notifications and setting focus mode profiles help you not fall back into old habits. After all, we have learned about how these apps work, and it is the best thing we can do for ourselves. However, as we learned in this chapter, it does not mean we should disconnect or abandon friends. We talked about the importance of texting, calling, and in-person meetings for those who had more trouble with these apps and desired to stay off in a much more permanent way while staying connected to those who matter. We began to appreciate that staying in contact and close does not mean returning to social media. Often, social media is a mirage.

We took a moment to talk about the impact of social media in a much more profound and detailed way. I decided to do this here so that we remember why we cannot just return to how things were, how the psychological and physical effects of social media use are natural and by design. The discussion here is different from chapter one because of our focus on experience and detail. In that discussion, we learned about technostress. Technostress bears physical and mental symptoms that are no different from those caused by chronic stress. We also learned about another insidious consequence of digital technology use: time pressure. We had to talk about why that was different from procrastinating and why it matters for our professional and personal lives. We also noted that time pressure is antithetical to happiness.

Chapter six dealt with a problem that many are looking at digital minimalism raise. They often think or say that a life like this is boring. We had to show them where they were worn and why digital minimalism did not equate to boring. In this chapter, we talked about the importance of adopting high-value activities instead of low-value activities. The distinction between the two is decided by purely economic means; there is nothing snobby about it. High valuer activities make the most economic sense while low-value activities do not. We also noted that not all activities are inherently one or another. However, they have a bias towards one or another.

According to our different situations, one may be more tur than the other for us. Then we explored activities that are almost always high value and talked about why they fit that description. I wanted you to find some for your own, so you cannot just live a fun life but one full and vibrant.

The final chapter was dedicated to how we can use technology to work for us instead of against us. We learned about the importance of a second brain, as the system of organizing and collecting information that makes up for all your brain's weaknesses. We saw how this could supercharge your creativity and maintain consistency and accuracy across all projects. We saw how such a habit would help you grow faster and live more within a small amount of time—allowing you to get the most out of your experiences.

That is what this book was. What it does for you is up to what you do with it. Go on, live life fully!

Kai

* * *

THANK YOU

I would like to really thank you for reading my book till the end, and most importantly, apply as much as you can from what you learned here. As nothing would make me happier than knowing that someone's life is getting better because of something I shared!

I consider myself leveraged because you chose my book over all the other books to discover.

So, THANK YOU for purchasing this book and for making it all the way to here.

Before you leave, I would like to ask for a favour! **Could you please share one or two things you learned or liked about this book in a review? That would really help me continue sharing more knowledge and would show your support to an independent author like myself!**

Your opinion will assist and encourage me to keep writing and publishing useful content to more people, hoping to make more people happier and enjoy their dream lives. Hearing from you would mean so much to me.

>> Leave a review on Amazon US <<

>> Leave a review on Amazon UK <<

REFERENCES

Addiction Policy Forum. (2020, September 20). *DSM-5 Criteria for Addiction Simplified.* https://www.addictionpolicy.org/post/dsm-5-facts-and-figures

Barret, L. F. (2018). *How Emotions Are Made.* Pan Books Ltd.

Baterna, Q. (2021, October 12). *What Is Surveillance Capitalism?* MUO. https://www.makeuseof.com/what-is-surveillance-capitalism/

Boroon, L., Abedin, B., & Erfani, E. (2021). The Dark Side of Using Online Social Networks. *Journal of Global Information Management, 29*(6), 1–21. https://doi.org/10.4018/jgim.20211101.oa34

Britannica. (2019). Twitter | History, Description, & Uses. In *Encyclopædia Britannica.* https://www.britannica.com/topic/Twitter

Chiappetta, M. (2017). The Technostress: definition, symptoms and risk prevention. *Sense & Sciences*, *4*, 358–361. https://doi.org/10.14616/sands-2017-1-358361

Fecther, J. (2015, September 27). *7 Benefits Of Reading Literary Fiction You May Not Know*. Lifehack. https://www.lifehack.org/307436/7-benefits-reading-literary-fiction-you-may-not-know-2

Fry, A. (2020, September 17). *Stress and insomnia*. Sleep Foundation. https://www.sleepfoundation.org/insomnia/stress-and-insomnia

Hall, M. (2021). Facebook. In *Encyclopædia Britannica*. https://www.britannica.com/topic/Facebook

Hoffman, H. (2008, October 8). *Four reasons why Facebook is succeeding in social networking*. CNET. https://www.cnet.com/culture/four-reasons-why-facebook-is-succeeding-in-social-networking/#:~:text=Simplicity%3A%20A%20lot%20of%20Facebook%27s%20success%20is%20due

Lyubomirsky, S. (2008). *The how of happiness : a scientific approach to getting the life you want*. Penguin Press.

Medina, J. (2014). *Brain rules for baby : how to raise a smart and happy child from zero to five.* Brunswick, Melbourne, Vic. Scribe Publications.

Moore, D. A., & Tenney, E. R. (2012). Time Pressure, Performance, and Productivity. *Research on Managing Groups and Teams,* 305–326. https://doi.org/10.1108/s1534-0856(2012)0000015015

Pew Research Center. (2021, April 7). *Mobile Fact Sheet.* Pew Research Center: Internet, Science & Tech; Pew Research Center. https://www.pewresearch.org/internet/fact-sheet/mobile/

Pinker, S. (2015). *How the mind works.* Penguin Books.

Psychology Today. (n.d.). *Default Mode Network | Psychology Today.* Www.psychologytoday.com. https://www.psychologytoday.com/us/basics/default-mode-network

Scott, PhD, E. (2020, February 29). *Stress From Work and Money Can Damage Your Sex Life.* Verywell Mind. https://www.verywellmind.com/how-stress-can-lead-to-low-libido-3145029#:~:text=When%20stress%20is%20chronic%2C%20the%20body%20uses%20sex

Scott, E. (2008, February 8). *6 Ways to Cope With Loneliness.*

Verywell Mind; Verywellmind. https://www.verywellmind.com/how-to-cope-with-loneliness-3144939

Shaw, E. (2018, November 19). *10 Wonderful Benefits of Traveling*. Dumb Little Man. https://www.dumblittleman.com/benefits-of-traveling/#:~:text=%2010%20Wonderful%20Benefits%20of%20Traveling%20%201

Theodore. (2020, April 8). *Skinner's box experiment - practical psychology*. Practical Psychology. https://practicalpie.com/skinners-box-experiment/

Tiwari, S. C. (2013). Loneliness: A disease? *Indian Journal of Psychiatry*, *55*(4), 320. https://doi.org/10.4103/0019-5545.120536

University of Rochester Medical Center. (2019). *Stress Can Increase Your Risk for Heart Disease - Health Encyclopedia - University of Rochester Medical Center*. Rochester.edu. https://www.urmc.rochester.edu/encyclopedia/content.aspx?ContentTypeID=1&ContentID=2171

Walker, M. P. (2018). *Why we sleep : unlocking the power of sleep and dreams*. Scribner, An Imprint Of Simon & Schuster, Inc.

What has the iPhone done to our lives? | Center

for Mobile Communication Studies. (n.d.). Sites.bu.edu. Retrieved May 3, 2022, from https://sites.bu.edu/cmcs/2017/11/16/what-has-the-iphone-done-to-our-lives/?msclkid=a0fadd17b5fb11ecadb365078420670e

Wheelwright, T. (2020, February 11). *Cell Phone Behavior Survey: Are People Addicted to Their Phones?* Reviews.org. https://www.reviews.org/mobile/cell-phone-addiction/

Whitten, A. (2017, March 17). *Why Stress Causes Fatigue and How To Overcome Stress*. The Energy Blueprint. https://theenergyblueprint.com/stress-causes-fatigue/#:~:text=It%20goes%20something%20like%20this%3A%20The%20adrenal%20glands

Wood, W. (2021). *GOOD HABITS, BAD HABITS : the science of making positive changes that stick*. Macmillan.

Made in the USA
Middletown, DE
17 November 2022

15373967R00094